HAUNTED

A Guide to Indiana's

HOOSIER

Famous Folklore and Spooky Sites

TRAILS

WANDA LOU WILLIS

CLERISY PRESS

HAUNTED HOOSIER TRAILS

For information contact:

CLERISY PRESS
c/o Keen Communications
PO Box 43673
Birmingham, AL 35243
www.clerisypress.com

ISBN 978-1-57860-115-8
Library of Congress Catalogue Card Number 2002111437

Cover design by Lloyd Brooks, Thrive, Inc.
Text and layout design by April Altman Reynolds
Maps and illustrations by Steven D. Armour
Cover photograph by Mike Fender

Printed and bound in the United States of America

For my parents, Ethel and Raymond Willis—
I hear the mockingbird sing;
the black-eyed china doll smiles;
I am the keeper of the dream.

And for my brothers, Chester and Donald.

Contents

Acknowledgments

Throughout the process of compiling and writing this book I was constantly reminded of the Hoosier warmth, and friendliness.

A very special thanks to my friends, Eric Mundell, Madonna Snyder, Bob and Carolyn Schmidt, Bill and Berky Davis and Tom Castaldi.

There are two other very special individuals who derserve recognition. Joy, my Belgian shepherd, who more than anyone else was my slave driver unfailingly awakening me at 2:00 AM each morning. And my dear friend, Nelson Price, who was always there with caring friendship, support and enthusiasm. If Joy got me up, Nelson kept me going. Much love to both of you.

❋❋❋

My sincere thanks to the following people for supplying information on local ghosts to supplement the hundreds of hours of historical research among old newspapers and county histories:

The Mason Long House:
Laura McCaffrey, present homeowner
Charlie Roduta, Fort Wayne *News-Sentinel* reporter

The Pfeiffer House:
Clark Valentine, present homeowner
Cindy Lauer, Pfeiffer House chef
Charlie Roduta

The Phantom of the Embassy:
Steven M. Toor, Embassy Theater House Staff Chairperson
Charlie Roduta

The Manitou Monster:
Shirley Willard, President, Fulton County Historical Society

Sister Sarah:
Bob Bradway, former homeowner
Marilyn French, retired reporter
Shirley Willard

Merbrink Cottage—The Winona Lake House of Love:
Marge Priser, Kosciusko Historical Society

Norm Hagg, General Manager, Editor-in-Chief, Warsaw *Time Union*

The Ghosts of "I" Street:
Jim Rodgers, Curator, La Porte County Historical Museum

Paukooshuck's Ghost:
Shirley Willard
Joan Dugger, Historian, Culver Antiquarium & Historical Society
Linda Rippey, Executive Director, Marshall County Historical Society

Child's Play:
Dr. John Johnson, owner of the Inn at Aberdeen
Irline Holley, Portage Public Library

Osceola Poltergeist:
Sean Walton, Reference Librarian, St. Joseph County Public Library

Oscar, The Beast of Busco:
Susan Richey, Whitley County Historical Society

Things go Bump in a Grand Manor—Hazelcot Castle:
Susan Richey

The White Hall Tavern:
Don Dunaway, Franklin County Historian

The Plantation Club's Hoodlums and Haunts:
Michael and Doni Nickerson, owners of Casio's Restaurant

Sam Maag . . . is it You?:
Toni R. Hepfer, present homeowner

"Good Night, Mr. 'G'":
Beth E. Oljace, Anderson Public Library

Miss Robert's Mansion:
Mr. Charles Sanqunetti, present homeowner

The Acton Mystery:
Sylvia C. Henricks, Vice President, Franklin Township, Marion County Historical Society

The Slippery Noodle:
Hal Yeagy, Jr., Owner

The Peek-A-Boo Ghost:
Bill and Berky Davis, present homeowners

Locust Hill:
Dave and Dixie Arnold, present homeowners

The Ultimate Long Distance Call:
Mary Margaret Lacoli, Vigo County Public Library

The Azalia Bridge:
Jennifer Gearries, Director, Bartholomew County Historical Society

The Laughery Creek Road Massacre:
Chris McHenry, Lawrenceburg Public Library District

Blue Balls of Light:
Ben Schneider, reporter
Dave B. Floyd, County Historian

The Legend of Poor Pollie: Linton's Beloved Eccentric:
Mary Witte, researcher

Hush Little Baby, Don't You Cry,
The Medora Haunted House,
The Witch of White Chapel:
Charlotte Sellers, Jackson County Public Library

Dark Hollow,
Purple Head Bridge,
The Spirit of Otter Pond,
The Coal Miner's Ghosts:
Richard Day, Research Assistant, Vincennes University Library

The Light at the End of the Tunnel:
Zach Merchant, Reference Assistant, Bedford Public Library
Sue Medland, Librarian, Mitchell Public Library

Paoli's Bluebeard:
Ann Colbert, Journalism Coordinator, Indiana University-Purdue University at Fort Wayne

The Ghost Rider of River Road,
Vengeance is Mine, Saith the Lord:
Debbie Siebert

What's Going on at the Tell City Library?:
Debbie Siebert, Librarian, Tell City Public Library
Paul Sanders, Assistant Director, Tell City Public Library
Kay Siebert, Bookmobile Director, Tell City Public Library
Brandi Sanders, Bookmobile Assistant, Tell City Public Library

Flat Creek Terror,
The Gullick House Ghost:
Sandy McBeth, Historian

Poor Mary,
Day is Done, Gone the Sun:
Jeannie Noe Carlisle, Historian

A Gentle Presence:
Lisa Fisher, present homeowner
Ellyn R. Kern, informant

The Ditney Man:
Rod Spaw, informant

The Pekin Ghost:
Pam French, owner

Some of these spooky sites belong to private owners. You may drive by, but please don't ask the present homeowners to tour you.

Northern Indiana

ALLEN COUNTY

Created in 1823 the county was named for Colonel John Allen, a Kentucky lawyer and Indian fighter who aided in the liberation of Fort Wayne in 1812 when Tecumseh, the Shawnee Chief, laid siege to the fort. This was the last serious threat from the Indians. The county comprises a good deal of northeastern Indiana.

Fort Wayne was platted and designated the county seat in 1824 and named for General Anthony Wayne, who built the first American fort after defeating Little Turtle in 1794 on the site of the important portage of the Maumee and St. Mary's Rivers. Other variant names for Fort Wayne have been Kekionga (blackberry patch), Fort Miami, French Town, Kisakon, Miami Town, Omee Town, Post Miami, and Twightwee Village. In the nineteenth century the town attracted industrialists, bankers and civic leaders who made the city a model of progressive thought and action. Its 1902 beaux arts courthouse is considered to be one of the finest examples of that style of architecture in the world and has recently been restored.

Fort Wayne is the hometown of actresses Carole Lombard and Shelley Long. Other famous individuals who have lived there are Wendy's founder Dave Thomas, designer Bill Blass, and television inventor Philo T. Farnsworth. Today it is the second largest city in the state, a center of industry and commerce, and Allen County is home of national corporate headquarters and automobile-related attractions.

The Mason Long House

It was 1965 when Laura and Ralph McCaffrey moved into their new home at 922 Columbia Avenue. The neighbors welcomed them, not with apple pies, but with whispered warnings! "The house is haunted."

They smiled indulgently. Ghosts? During nearly forty years of living in the Long house, the McCaffreys have changed their minds. They're convinced that they've been sharing their house with the Mason Long family, including the "dust kitten," the name they've given to the spirit of the family cat.

The McCaffreys really don't mind sharing space with their friendly ghosts and "would never want to get rid of them." Laura McCaffrey said in a recent interview, "They are the ambience of the house."

In 1892 Mason Long could well afford to lavish money on building his Columbia Avenue home. He hadn't been born into wealth or a respected station in life, but had worked hard to achieve success.

Long came to Fort Wayne in 1865, but his pre-Summit City life had been harsh and painful. An only child, he was born September 10, 1842 in a small town in Licking County, Ohio. Just before young Mason's seventh birthday, his father died. Later in his life Long looked back on those times with his mother as being a rare interlude filled with love and happiness.

Four years after the loss of his father, his beloved mother died and he moved in with the only remaining relative who could care and provide for an orphan.

When the relative passed on, Mason became a ward of the county. A German farmer agreed to take him as an indentured servant—a farmhand. The sad and lonely boy worked hard for his board and food. Often, evidently, it wasn't hard enough and he would be whipped, making him rebellious and causing even more severe punishment.

As the Civil War came, the young man ran away to join the Union army. In camp he learned many things which would get him through life, including card playing. Once the war was over he used this talent to become a very successful professional gambler.

Back in Fort Wayne he opened the Long Hotel—a lodging house, tavern and gambling casino where he was one of his own best customers at both the games table and the bar. Then, with the deal of a card he lost everything—or at least he thought he had.

With no money and nowhere to go, he became a Christian and shortly thereafter he wrote his biography *The Life of Mason Long, the Converted Gambler*. Traveling on the preaching circuit, he condemned the evils of gambling and drinking, becoming a popular and much-sought-after speaker.

Now on the "straight and narrow," Long flourished as a businessman. George Pixley, a clothier and banker who came to Fort Wayne from Utica, New

York in 1876, entered into a partnership with Long in a brokerage firm. The partners purchased a lot at East Berry and Court Streets and in 1889 constructed a five-story office and commercial building, the Pixley-Long Building.

In his later years, Long enjoyed a family, a lucrative business and respect. With pride he watched the workmen constructing a grand two-story home with fourteen rooms. The house embodied everything he'd always dreamed of.

Never able to lose the hard-work habits of his youth, this reformed gambler and drinker continued to work harder than he should have, and in 1903 Mason Long was stricken with "apoplexy"—a stroke. With his wife and children at his bedside he died.

Though Long and his family are all long since deceased, they haven't left their Columbia Avenue home, according to Laura and Ralph McCaffrey, who now own the mansion. The house becomes "noisy" with activity or celebration during the Christmas holidays and in August and October.

At least that's how Mrs. McCaffrey explains the alterations that take place in the house. The shades of the lights change. Whether it's the sunlight filtering through the windows or a lamp lit in the evening, the rooms suddenly take on a mellow, muted glow. And at those times the hallway seems to be filled with foggy shapes.

Whatever shares the living space with the McCaffreys affects even their dog. He'll run to the door standing there with his tail wagging as if to greet a visitor—but nobody's there. And then there's the "dust kitten," which moves about like a ball of dust when a light breeze disturbs it.

Every now and then, McCaffrey says she catches a whiff of an old-fashioned floral fragrance she believes might have been worn by Mrs. Long.

The acceleration of "activity" during the month of August is a mystery. But it can be certain it held—and still does—some significance to the Long family. Perhaps they still celebrate the change in their father's life which took him from dissipation to respectability.

No matter how much "noise" or activity the Long family ghosts create, they and the McCaffreys are happy together.

When the McCaffreys moved into the Mason Long house, 922 Columbia Ave., they were warned, "The house is haunted."

Photo by Bob Schmidt

The Pfeiffer House

There is nothing unusual about the Charles Pfeiffer house that would draw attention to it. This warm and inviting, red brick three-story structure—now a restaurant at 434 W. Wayne Street owned by Clark Valentine—is solid, sturdy and comfortable, much like the family who'd lived there in the mid-1800s. The Pfeiffers: Charles, Henrietta and their two children, Fred and Marguerite, were contented inhabitants. After he grew up and entered the family business and his parents were gone, bachelor Fred Pfeiffer maintained the house outside and inside, much as it had been during his childhood. Fred Pfeiffer died in 1995, after having lived in the same house just shy of one hundred years.

Fred had been the heir to business interests in Fort Wayne ranging from meatpacking to the Lincoln National Bank, of which his father was one of the co-founders. Through years of single-minded dedication, he had increased the fortune, and at his death his estate was valued at ten million dollars, 80 percent of which was left to various charities. His niece and nephew shared equally in the remaining estate.

Now Fred seems to appear for Clark Valentine, the present owner. Is he unwilling to leave the home he occupied for so long? Clark and his chef, Cindy Lauer, report hearing the doorbell ring; however, upon checking, finding nobody there.

Clark had been introduced to both Fred and the house in 1989, when he began handling the aging man's financial affairs as a surety officer for the Lincoln National Bank. Valentine knew the old gentleman as an intelligent, shrewd businessman owning large tracts of real estate, stocks and bonds. Though there were several years difference in their ages, the two became good friends. Clark was well aware of Fred's total commitment and love for his home. "Fred wanted to keep everything the same," he had told a reporter during an interview. "It was very important to him."

That's why, when Fred died, Clark decided to purchase the house he had come to admire. His new residence was as it had been when Fred lived there, complete with two fireplaces and beautiful hand-hewn woodwork. The family piano and Louis XVI style furniture still stand in the exact same position where they had stood for one hundred years. He decided to make only necessary repairs and clean the home. He and his daughter, Sara, entered into a partnership and opened the house as a restaurant named, aptly, the Pfeiffer House.

The attic room, where Fred and sister Marguerite used to play and ride their bicycles, is now a comedy improv theater with an odd ambience pervading its gabled corners. Realizing the interest—or curiosity—the community has in the house and the family, Clark will agree to conduct infrequent tours.

He remembers giving a group of women a tour of the house. They were on the second floor and were about to go to the attic area, when one of the women refused to go any farther, nervously retreating to the first floor. She later confided that she'd felt a presence and became frightened.

The chef, Cindy Lauer, agrees that a presence has often been felt in the old home. She has been in the habit of arriving early—before the boss, his daughter or the servers—to get things "cooking." It's in these lonely, early morning hours when the house is still and the doors locked that the chef can feel a presence. Steps will echo on the stairs. If she moves to the hallway and looks up the stairs she sees no one, and yet will sense that someone is looking down at her.

She also reports odd happenings in the kitchen—pots sliding off counters and other disturbances.

A server has reported setting up the tables for the lunch crowd and hearing doors opening and closing upstairs, as if someone was going from room to room. The chef was the only other person in the house and she was in the kitchen.

Doors slam. Salt and pepper shakers suddenly fall from the tables. Lights go on and off by themselves.

Clark Valentine likes to think that Fred Pfeiffer has returned to the home he was so fond of and was so reluctant to leave, even in death.

Those who knew him believe that Fred Pfeiffer still walks through the home he loved and lived in for nearly one hundred years.

Photo by Bob Schmidt

The Phantom of the Embassy

The excitement could be felt like the electrical charged air just before a lightning-filled thunderstorm. A thunderous sound—and then—rising from the darkness below, the magnificent Page pipe organ would come into view, accompanied by the eighteen-piece orchestra. Music filled the theater and the show began. For a few cents a theatergoer could escape reality and revel in the luxury of theatrical performances for a couple of hours.

It was the 1920s when the theater first opened, the era of extravagant opulent movie and vaudevillian palaces. The 3,000-seat theater at 125 W. Jefferson Street first billed itself as the Emboyd, a name given it by W. C. Quimby, the manager, to honor his mother Emily Boyd. French marble trim covered the walls, an Italian vaulted ceiling soared above them, and mirrors on the landing reflected patrons as they ascended the grand staircase beneath five-foot sconces glittering with crystal spangles. Moorish styled pillars led to the vestibule of the gentlemen's lounge, which included a fireplace decorated with an intricate, ornate plaster sculpture.

Bud Berger believed himself lucky when he was hired as the Emboyd's first stage manager. He took his responsibilities seriously, making certain he was at the theater and ready to assist the director during rehearsals and performances long before anyone else arrived. He'd stay long after everyone else had gone home, reviewing every detail, checking every prop. One job that he paid particular attention to was managing the lights around the stage, and especially the ghost light, the subdued spotlight above the stage that allowed the vaudeville performers to find their places without tripping. Bud was fascinated by it all and it became his life. He had fallen in love with the Emboyd.

His days—and nights—were spent almost entirely at the theater. It occurred to him that he could be more readily available by fixing a place to sleep under the stage. He'd be there whenever he was needed, and he could guard his beloved theater at all times. His employers gave him permission.

Bud was friendly and well liked by the many entertainers who trod the boards of the Emboyd's stage, such as Bob Hope, Donald O'Connor and Fort Wayne's own Marilyn Maxwell. The walls of the dressing-room area were decorated with his growing collection of autographed photos.

The Alliance Amusement Company bought the theater in 1952, changing the name to the Embassy Theater. It continued to operate primarily as a movie theater. And, even then, Bud slept there and tended the building.

Thirteen years later Bud left the theater at last—he died in 1965.

Without the love Bud had lavished on it, and in a downtown where times and theater-going habits were changing, the theater declined. The owners announced in 1972 that it would be more profitable to demolish the building and create a parking lot.

Bud's spirit of love for the Emboyd may have reached out from beyond the grave to touch the hearts of the community and raise the funds to save the old landmark. Steve Toor, Embassy management, feels strongly that Bud Berger rescued the theater. "He's a guardian-angel ghost," Toor believes. He is positive it was Bud who helped save the Embassy. "It was going to be torn down in sixty days. It was real close."

The Embassy Theater Foundation was created, and through its efforts the theater has been restored to its original beauty and is considered to be Indiana's largest and most opulent historic theater. Ballets, operas, the Fort Wayne Philharmonic Orchestra, concerts, Broadway Musical Series and theater organ popular music programs appear on its stage.

More than thirty years after his death Bud still seems to reside in the theater he loved more than any woman. Many have felt his presence. Toor and several employees believe he's responsible for doors suddenly closing and theater seats folding and unfolding.

This ghostly presence even likes to play a prank from time to time on the current stage manager. During a final stage check for a holiday presentation, the stage manager realized the Christmas tree was missing from the set. No one admitted to removing it. In a panic all stagehands searched frantically. Just before the curtain went up it was found in a place no one would have expected. Was Bud playing a prank?

Many who work in the theater say some of the incidents attributed to Bud can be easily explained; other occurrences are more mysterious.

There is one telling sign that he is around and about: Sometimes, late at night, the pipe organ will start playing. Whether one note or a melody—it's definitely Bud.

Bud Berger, stage manager for the elegant Embassy Theater, spent his days and nights in the theater. Even after death he seems to look after the theater and play the pipe organ.

Photo by Bob Schmidt

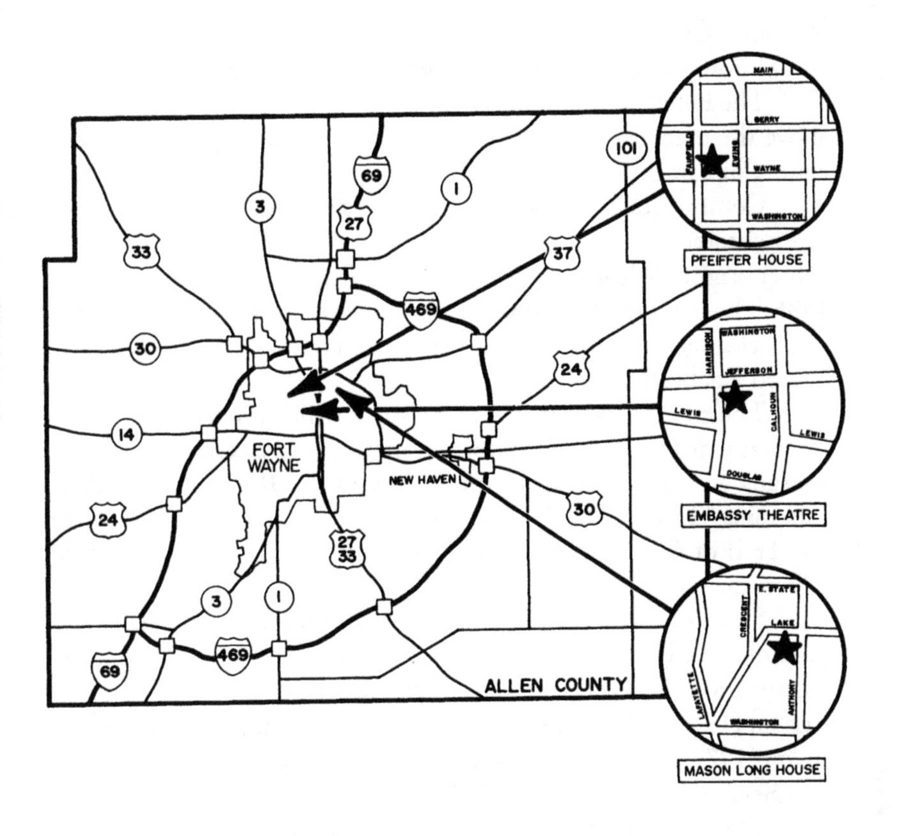

69
101
3
1
27
33
37
469
30
24
14
FORT WAYNE
NEW HAVEN
27
33
3
1
469
69
ALLEN COUNTY
MAIN
BERRY
FAIRFIELD
EWING
WAYNE
WASHINGTON
PFEIFFER HOUSE
WASHINGTON
HARRISON
JEFFERSON
LEWIS
CALHOUN
LEWIS
DOUGLAS
EMBASSY THEATRE
E. STATE
CRESCENT
LAKE
LAFAYETTE
ANTHONY
WASHINGTON
MASON LONG HOUSE

FULTON COUNTY

Fulton County, named for the inventor of the steamboat, Robert Fulton, was formed in 1835 and organized in 1836.

The Potawatomi Indians inhabited this area in a series of camps above the many lakes and rivers. The land was swampy, making the county one of the last to be settled in the state.

Commissioners appointed by the legislature designated the town of Rochester as the county seat. Alexander Chamberlain, a local mill owner originally from Rochester, New York, had laid out the town in 1835. The town's name probably was borrowed either from New York or Rochester, England, or possibly from another early mill owner named Rochester.

The county takes pride in its history, which is demonstrated by the many historical markers dotting the landscape. The Potawatomi Indians were removed from the county in the 1830s, to take their infamous "Trail of Death" west, now commemorated each fall with the Trail of Courage rendezvous at the Fulton County Historical Museum.

Some of the many famous citizens of Fulton County, past and present, are Clyde Beatty, wild animal trainer; Floyd J. (Jack) Mattice, who in 1903 became the first sports broadcaster in the nation; the first Tarzan (1918), Elmo Lincoln; and Dr. Otis Bowen, Governor of Indiana (1972–80), Cabinet member under President Ronald Reagan and Secretary of Health and Welfare.

The Indiana Department of Natural Resources, Division of Fish and Wildlife recognizes Fulton County as having seven good fishing lakes. Lake Manitou, 731 acres, is the largest lake in the county and supports a population of largemouth bass, bluegill, crappie and northern pike. Other fish which can be found in the lakes are yellow perch, hybrid stripe bass and smallmouth bass.

The Manitou Monster

Before the time men walked the earth, Indians believed there was a primeval era when strange and awful creatures existed. Perhaps it was their way of explaining the Age of Dinosaurs. Today they only remain in legends. Or do they?

Lake Manitou (from the Algonquian word ma-ne-to, meaning spirit or supernatural force), a 731-acre lake one mile east of Rochester, hides a secret—the Manitou Monster! According to an Indian legend, the lake was—and may still be—the home of Meshekenabek, a serpentlike water creature, much like that of Scotland's Loch Ness.

Before the white man came to the area, there was an Indian village near the lake. One day the Indians heard a great disturbance coming from the lake. The water became agitated and churning and waves rushed from the vortex lapping at the shore. With a thunderous heave a giant creature rose from the core of the maelstrom. Meshekenabek, the devil serpent!

Meshekenabek came out of the lake and wrought havoc on the village. One Indian, Messou's cousin, one of the village's finest young braves, was killed during the quaking event.

Fearfully the Indians watched the great hulk sink back into the depths of the lake. Then they saw Messou pushing his canoe into the churning waters. The whole village begged him to return. He didn't listen. He was intent on seeking vengeance on the creature that had killed his cousin. The villagers watched as he paddled toward the middle of the lake and disappeared.

The Indians had lived close to the lake and fished its waters for generations, but now they left, moving their villages away from the "dark lake," never to fish its waters again.

When the first white men came to the shores of Lake Manitou, they built a mill and a settlement. The Indians tried to warn them of the monster and the bad luck in the lake but to no avail. John Lindsay, the first blacksmith in the area, noticed a disturbance on the surface of the lake. He couldn't believe his eyes. It was a monster.

In recounting his tale he described the creature as a snakelike beast, about sixty feet long and dingy in color with large yellow spots. The head was about three feet across the frontal bone and had the shape of a cow's head. No one believed Lindsay. A few who heard the story commented that he must've been looking through a glass—a glass of whiskey.

In 1838 a boatload of men were fishing when they saw the monster and quickly rowed to shore. The description was the same as that of Lindsay's. This time someone did listen. The *Logansport Telegraph* reported the sighting. George Winters, the artist, sketched his conception of the monster for the *Telegraph* article, which was published August 11, 1838.

There was a great deal of talk about forming an expedition and making an attempt to capture the monster. The newspaper article "traveled" to New England's east coast where "men of the sea" offered their services. Some even came to the area bringing huge nets and whaling harpoons. But the monster refused to surface again. After several days they grew weary of waiting and returned to New England.

No more sightings were reported until 1849 when the *Logansport Journal* ran a headline: "The Devil Caught at Last." Could this be true? People traveled miles to just get a glimpse of Meshekenabek. The monster turned out to be a huge buffalo carp weighing several hundred pounds, with the head alone weighing thirty pounds. A few remaining Indians did not believe it was possible, insisting the monster was supernatural, unable to be caught by Indian or white men. The town became skeptical of the monster found.

Then in 1888 Phillip Cook caught a giant spoonbill catfish in the lake. It was so large he enlisted the aid of three others to help him bring it in. Once the fish was landed the men estimated its weight to be 116 pounds. Could this then be the real Lake Manitou Monster? For a time Cook exhibited the huge fish. Then he cut it up and sold it for ten cents a pound, at the time a high price. He had no problem selling the fish—it seems as if nearly everyone wanted to have a piece of the Manitou Monster.

There hasn't been a sighting in over a hundred years. But longtime residents whose families have lived in the area since the first sightings say that the Manitou Monster is still lurking in the depths of this largest lake in Fulton County. They and their relatives have heard a deep booming roar, especially in the quiet of winter nights.

Others will smile and shake their heads; "It's just the ice shifting on the lake."

We can all wonder.

❋❋❋

Sister Sarah

Silently she enters the room. As the man and his wife sleep she watches. Who are these people? Uninvited they and their children have moved into her *home as if they belong there.*

True, they haven't interrupted her nightly routines nor do they get in her way. Still she can't help wondering if they know this was her *house!*

The inhabitants of Sister Sarah's house described the apparition as a female with long hair, wearing a light-colored dress. She is more like a shadow than a real woman.

Bob Bradway had been looking for a house to buy. The old two-story farmhouse on Fort Wayne Road, east of County Road 825 East, not too far from Rochester, was just the place the family of seven needed. There was plenty of room for their five little girls to play both inside and outdoors. Nobody mentioned the house was haunted. It wouldn't have mattered anyway because the Bradways didn't believe in ghosts.

One day shortly after the family moved in, they were exploring the grounds when they noticed some pine trees in a field behind the house. Almost buried in the thick brush between the trees they discovered an old family cemetery. One of the stones bore the weathered inscription:

Sarah McIntire
Wife of R. McIntire
Died Nov. 4, 1873 at the age of 33

Not too long after that discovery they were first visited by the specter.

Often during the night when the children were in bed and the parents were relaxing downstairs, they'd hear someone walking upstairs. "It wasn't an old house's floor creaking." Bob said, "We heard footsteps." They accused all of the girls; everyone denied making the noise.

As the days turned into weeks the parents still heard someone walking upstairs long after the children had been put to bed. Late one night they heard a different noise. The door at the foot of the stairs leading to the second floor squeaked open. They then heard the familiar footsteps. Bob was certain that this time he would catch one of the girls.

Quietly he made his way up the stairs. He didn't encounter one of his children in the hallway but instead the ghost! Both stood looking at each other. Then the phantom disappeared like a puff of smoke.

After the parents discussed the sighting and after many nights of hearing someone walking across the upstairs floor they began referring to the ghost as Sister Sarah. They chose this name because of the name on the moldering tombstone nearly hidden in the pine trees.

"Whether she really is Sarah, that's something only the ghost would know. We named her Sister Sarah because she had become a part of the family," Bob explained. Sometimes she visited without materializing, appearing as a burst of warm air.

They never had any real problems with Sister Sarah. She didn't seem to be malicious or angry, just as much a part of the house as the floors she walked during the day and late at night or the squeaky door she felt compelled to open from time to time.

The only time Sarah made her displeasure known was when she overturned a Christmas tree one night. All the family was in bed asleep when they were awakened by the sound. Rushing downstairs they found the tree had been toppled over. Many of the ornaments and bulbs were broken. At first the family blamed the dog, but then they realized the dog was on the enclosed back porch where he usually spent the night. There's no explanation as to why Sarah would've knocked the tree down except perhaps it was in her way. After the broken glass was cleaned up, they righted the tree and moved it out of the phantom's path.

In 1962 the Bradways decided to adopt a one-and-a-half-year-old boy, Mike. As was the family's custom Mike's picture was added to the collection on the old boarded-up fireplace's mantel. Soon his picture was found lying face down on the floor. After this happened several times, they decided that Sarah didn't want the picture on display, so they put it in a drawer.

Of course, it could be she was trying to send another message. Since Mike was an adopted child she might have felt he was not a part of *her* family.

The family no longer lives in the house. Until they moved, they never told anyone about seeing Sister Sarah. "Back then, if you talked about things like that, people thought you were ready for the loony bin. Now I don't care what they say. If they want to believe, fine. If not, that's fine too." Bob further states that he'd be willing to take a lie detector test or swear on a stack of Bibles that what he's said is the truth. "We lived there and I know what we saw and heard. It's not imagination or made up. It happened."

The family who lives there today says nothing unusual has ever happened, nor have they ever heard anything strange. Some people believe that when children are in a place where a ghost might exist, this will stimulate ghostly activity and sightings such as experienced by the Bradways. Perhaps this is why Sister Sarah surfaced for the Bradways.

Some of the stories which have grown around Sister Sarah are bizarre themselves. Because she is called "Sister Sarah," one story states she was a nun who killed orphans, while another calls her a witch.

The tales about the grave seem older than the Bradways' sightings. One of them says Sarah was unwed and pregnant in a time when a young woman would be ostracized. Did the baby's father refuse to marry her, leaving her desolate and frightened? One folklore tradition says so.

The story goes that she remained at her parent's house, staying in her room, refusing to see anyone. Through her actions people in the town began to talk and speculate, looking on her as a fallen woman—a harlot! Eventually her friends ceased visiting for fear that by association they, too, would be judged. Did she kill herself?

She is obviously buried in a lone grave, far from the sanctuary of the churchyard. Other folktales say she was not an unwed mother, but an unfaithful wife carrying another man's child. In this scenario she jumped from the window to escape a fire set by her jealous husband. Another version of this story states that she had her baby. When her husband realized that the child did not look like him, he knew she'd been unfaithful. In a rage he killed the baby. Then he set the house on fire. Sarah escaped by jumping out of the upstairs window leaving her husband to die in the inferno.

Today it is said Sarah still haunts the gravesite, walking at night with a candle in her hand. Various methods have been devised to summon forth Sarah's spirit or to prove something eerie can happen at her grave. Call her name and she appears in a puff of smoke. Pour a glass of water over her grave. Leave the empty glass and return in a half-hour and the glass will be filled with blood.

Marilyn French, a reporter for the *Akron/Mentone News,* wrote an article about Sarah in November 1978. Recently Marilyn recalled going to the old cemetery as a teenager with a group of her friends. Remembering that night, with flashlights and a gang of kids pushing and shoving and screaming, her memory of the experience is somewhat chilling. No, she didn't see Sarah. However, as an adult she believes she and Sarah "met."

She revisited the graves in 1978 for photographs to accompany her article. "I took several pictures of the area, house and graves. Something funny happened when the film was developed. All the pictures came out except those of Sarah's tombstone. They were blank. I think I had to go back two or three more times. Each time the pictures were developed they came out blank. Finally I was able to get what I needed."

As she recounted those excursions, she admitted they had left her shaken. She began remembering how difficult it was to even write the story. "Every time I sat down to the typewriter and began to type, it would turn off all by itself. I'd turn it on again. And, it would turn off. This happened so many times I almost gave up. I thought Sarah didn't want me to write about her. Finally I was able to complete it. But, I can tell you, I was pretty unnerved by the time it was done."

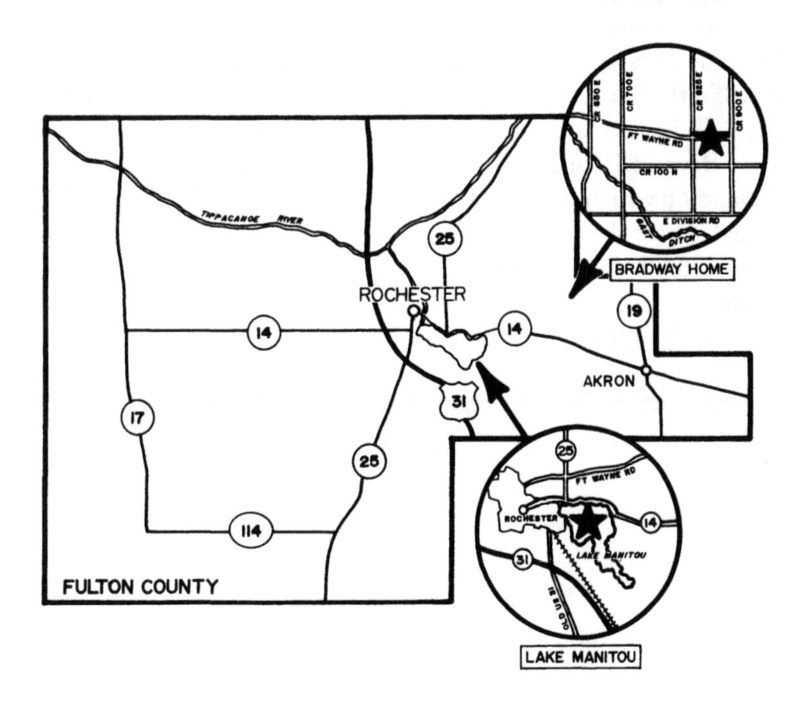

HUNTINGTON COUNTY

In 1831 a city was established on the site of a Miami village, Wepecheange, "place of flints." That same year General John Tipton purchased the land and the following year Huntington County was formed. Tipton had a town platted on his land in 1833 and then offered a portion to the county for use as the county seat.

Both the city and the county were named for Samuel Huntington, a Connecticut delegate to the Continental Congress and signer of the Declaration of Independence.

At Roanoke on July 4, 1835, the Wabash and Erie Canal was officially opened from Fort Wayne to the Dickey Lock, approximately fifteen miles west of Fort Wayne. While the canal's success was short-lived, its path followed the prime right-of-way through the area, and in 1856 the Wabash Railroad laid its tracks along the old canal tow-path. Today US 24 runs along that same route.

Beyond Roanoke, just 1.7 miles east on US 24, can be seen a depression which is one of the last remnants of the Wabash and Erie Canal. Once the longest artificial waterway in North America, the canal extended 464 miles between Toledo, Ohio, and Evansville, Indiana.

Today Huntington County is primarily agricultural.

The Haunting of Canal House

A member of the Indiana Canal Society was investigating the only visible reminder of the Wabash and Erie Canal just 1.7 miles east of Roanoke on US 24—a depression in the land where the canal lock had been. While intent on mentally picturing how the canal looked back in the mid-1800s, he heard someone call out for help. He spent several minutes looking around and found no one in need of assistance. Deciding teenagers where having fun with him, he returned to Fort Wayne.

At one of the Canal Society's meetings he told another member about the Roanoke site and then laughingly described to him the prank supposedly played on him by area teenagers. The man, a lifelong resident of the Roanoke area, told him that it had not been a hoax. What he had heard could have been one of the ghosts connected with the farmhouse which once sat along the canal. And therein, of course, lies a tale.

The opening of the Wabash and Erie Canal increased commerce to Roanoke, which is just fifteen miles west of Fort Wayne.

Lorenzo "Van" VanBecker's farm one mile north of the village of Roanoke bordered the canal and afforded opportunities to increase his wealth. This successful farmer had just moved his family into a new, impressive, two-story white house with green shutters above the canal lock.

Passengers sharing cramped space with cargo, cattle and hogs, traders, land speculators, settlers, and a few unsavory individuals all seeking opportunities in the newly acquired lands could see the house as they approached on the canal and looked at it as a convenient "getting off" place. Van and his wife often offered board and meals to the weary travelers.

Just below the hill where his grand house sat Van built a boatyard to meet the need for more canal boats. This was, after all, the "canal age." Once a boat was completed and until it was purchased, he would fit it out with a crew and operate the boat between Roanoke and Fort Wayne.

Though the canals brought the promise of prosperity, they also brought death: malaria, typhoid and yellow fever. The humid heat of summer made it worse. Many workers, passengers and those who served them became ill, VanBecker's wife among them.

He realized that if he were to continue providing lodging and meals for travelers, he needed a housekeeper. He offered the job to Mariah Heddwick, about whom he knew virtually nothing except that she had the reputation of being one of the finest cooks on the Wabash and Erie. There were those, however, who thought her a bit odd. From being considered odd to being considered dangerous, maybe even a witch, was a short jump in the 1840s.

VanBecker was a drinking man, as were many of the men who worked for him. James Furman, the orphan son of his neighbors, was an exception. Van never tried to force liquor on the boy, but when he and his men sat down to enjoy more than a few, he'd hand the boy a coin, saying it was no more than right that he should have some reward, as they did.

In the winter James would chop wood; in summer he'd work in the boatyard. After completion of the *Nettie Cook*, VanBecker turned to the young boy James and said, "Well, do you think you'd like to be a part of the crew for the shipment of hogs to Fort Wayne?"

For a time after the boat had left the yard, the mules slowly walking the tow path pulling the boat along, the small group was quiet. One of the men, Coyle, was the first to break the silence. "Well, James, how do you like working for Van?"

"Just fine," he answered.

The men looked at each other. Then John Trichett blurted out, "Ah, hell. Let's get it over with. Boy, have you heard or seen anything strange up at the big house that you couldn't explain? Well, keep alert, boy. Some say the house is haunted." During the rest of the trip the story was told.

It was true VanBecker's wife had been ill. She needed nursing. Mariah Heddwick had just arrived by boat. She sought out Van and said she'd heard his wife was ill. She explained that she'd survived the illness and thought she could help his wife do the same. Van was thankful for the help and hired her.

But, instead of getting better his wife took a turn for the worse and within three days under Mariah's care, she was dead.

People began to talk. It didn't appear to them that VanBecker's wife had been near death's door before Mariah began taking care of her. Had Mariah poisoned her, wanting to seize an opportunity to live in a fine house and in time become its new mistress?

After their return from Fort Wayne, the men returned to their duties on the canal and at the boatyard. James Furman stayed in the big house, sharing his bedroom with two other workers, Joe and Aleck. One night they all heard moaning and shrieking. It had really frightened Aleck. He'd jumped clear out of his bed and stood whimpering in the corner. The next day Aleck packed up and left without saying a word to anybody.

During his second winter at the VanBecker farm James Furman, after chopping wood, was warming himself in front of the fireplace, alone in the room. Van was down at the boat dock, Mariah in another part of the house. Suddenly he heard somebody outside call out in distress. He hurried to the door and flung it open. Not a soul was in sight. He didn't doubt his ears. He knew what he'd heard.

Confused and concerned, he went in search of Mariah and found her in the kitchen. "Did you hear something?" he demanded. She didn't seem the least bit surprised and merely said, "Oh, that. Why that's common around this house. I hear it often. The house is supposed to be haunted, you know."

"So we've heard," he murmured.

One day a young land seeker from Starke County arrived on a canal packet. When he was told that sometimes travelers were given lodging at the big white house, the young man decided to disembark, stay overnight and next morning look for land.

Van told James that the young land seeker was going to stay and share James' room.

The next morning the young man from Starke County was gone. Mariah said he'd left early, saying he was going to walk into Roanoke to see what he could find out about land sales.

Some weeks later the parents and fiancée of the Starke County man arrived at the boatyard. They'd traced him to this point and could find out nothing else. No one in Roanoke had seen him.

Finally they had to believe that he was dead. Perhaps he'd been jumped on the road to Roanoke, killed and robbed of the money sewn inside his vest and coat.

About this same time James Furman noticed Van was very nervous and drinking more than usual. He seemed to dread being in his fine, big, white house, especially at night. Often he'd spend his nights in the old house up the hill, shunning the canal house.

One day while they were all down at the boatyard Van left to go up to the white house. Quite some time had passed and Van hadn't returned.

James decided to go look for him. The house was deathly quiet. He called out first to Van and then Mariah. No one answered. Searching the first floor rooms he found no one.

With more than a bit of nervousness he climbed the stairs. The housekeeper's room was at the head of the landing. Knocking on the door he received no response. Cautiously he opened the door. The room was empty.

The door to VanBecker's room was ajar. With his heart pounding he slowly pushed it open. All he could see was a pool of blood!

He ran down the stairs and out of the house as fast as he could calling out to the others for help. After what seemed hours they finally gave up the search for Van and the housekeeper, Mariah. They were never seen again. Their mysterious disappearance was never solved, nor was an explanation given for the pool of blood. James wondered if the young land seeker's disappearance was a part of the mystery surrounding the house. And what about the ghost of the wife? Had she been seeking retribution and found it in the grim disappearance of Van and Mariah?

The boatyard was closed and the farm was sold; James moved on to other things. The property was for sale within a short time. And again the new owners were thrilled with the farm and the beautiful white house on the hill. However, they didn't stay in the house very long before they, too, moved out. Everyone believed that the big house on the hill above the canal was truly haunted. Both owners had reported hearing moaning, shrieking and pleas for help. The blood stains in the upper bedroom never faded. The newest owners tried to sell the farm, but no one wanted it. Finally they moved away, leaving the white house on the hill empty. Or was it?

The fragile deteriorating house was still standing in 1928 when an old man called "Uncle Jimmy," shortly before he died, told a *Huntington Herald Press* reporter the story of the haunted canal house. He knew it was true. He'd worked for Lorenzo "Van" VanBecker. He had heard the moaning, shrieking and pleas for help. His name was James Furman.

The canal is gone, long gone, a tragic failure and loss of money when the railroad era came in. Today all that's left of that era is a depression in the land where the canal lock had been. There have been a few reports of people hearing someone calling out in distress. But no one is there.

❋❋❋

KOSCIUSKO COUNTY

Kosciusko County, organized in 1836, was named for Thaddeus Kosciusko, a Polish national hero and aide-de-camp to General George Washington. Kosciusko has the distinction of being the fourth largest county in the state as well as being the location of more than one hundred lakes. The 2,720-acre Lake Wawasee, which was named for the Miami Indian Chief Wau-wa-aus-see, originally called Turkey Lake, is Indiana's largest natural lake. The deepest is Lake Tippecanoe.

The county seat, Warsaw, incorporated in 1854, and named for the capital of Poland, is a summer playground for thousands who flock there to enjoy swimming, fishing and boating.

Winona Lake, first known as Eagle Lake because its shape resembled an eagle with outspread wings, has been a church-oriented community. Evangelist Billy Sunday and singer Homer Rodeheaver were among its many famous visitors.

The Kosciusko County Courthouse received nationwide attention in 1921 during a six-day trial of the Culver Bank bandits. Clarence Darrow of Chicago defended the four men, who were sentenced to life imprisonment for the robbery and the murder of a police officer.

Kosciusko's Creighton Brothers Hatchery produces more than 3.2 million dozen eggs per year. Because of this industry's large output, the Warsaw and Mentone area is known as the Egg Basket of the Midwest.

The Fish That Got Away

This is a story about the "big one" that got away—and it's true!

It was the summer of 1956. Henry was ready for a day of sport fishing at Silver Lake, twelve miles south of Warsaw. He wasn't ready for what got hooked on his light tackle.

He had chosen a spot on the north end of the lake, where other fishermen in the vicinity were all intent on a pleasurable day of angling. Henry contemplated catching a few good-sized bluegills. Around 9 AM his line received a strong tug, indicating that he had a pretty large fish to reel in. He didn't realize this tug was going to result in nearly fourteen hours of battle between man and fish, and that the fish would win!

People began gathering on the banks as it became apparent that Henry had indeed caught himself a big one. They wanted to be there when it finally was landed to see what type of fish he'd caught. Would it be a record catch?

The battle between man and fish continued with speculation and verbal bets traveling through the groups that continued to gather and swell as the day wore on. WRSW began broadcasting news about the intense struggle going on at Silver Lake, capturing the imagination of thousands of listeners across northern Indiana. People jammed the switchboard, phoning in their own fish stories or suggestions as to what kind of fish, or thing, Henry had caught. The story and pictures were front-page news for the *Warsaw Times-Union.*

Several curious folk drove to Silver Lake to watch the struggle. Members of the Lake Conservation Club, the Grant County Emergency Squad, the Silver Lake Fire Department and the Indiana Conservation Department soon joined them. For the fishermen in the crowd the struggle became all that more exciting when they learned Henry was using only a three-pound line. A great deal of skill was required to keep the thin line from breaking.

Henry had been under siege for nearly four exhausting hours when the owner of the Silver Lake resort joined him in his boat and took over the fight, allowing Henry a rest. Henry received word one of his children had become ill and he needed to return home to Warsaw.

The sympathetic onlookers vowed they would not let his fish get away. They would continue the battle until he could return. The president of the conservation club stepped in for Henry, and with the resort owner, he proceeded to wage a nonstop battle with the fish for three more hours.

At that time two other competent fishermen relieved the pair. All in all the fish wore out four pairs of highly qualified fishermen and two nylon fishing lines before the end of the battle.

Seven hours into the battle there were no less than thirty-four boats surrounding Henry's. The captive fish took them on runs up and down Silver Lake numerous times. At the eighth hour the line finally broke. The alert fisherman at that time, however, grabbed the end of the line as it passed the tip of the pole and he began playing the fish by hand while another spinning rod and line was brought from shore. The pair managed to tie the new line onto the broken end of the original line and in that way were able to continue the fight. The next two hours the fishermen made an unsuccessful attempt to "herd" the monster to shallower water on the west side of the lake.

Henry returned just as night began. The fear of having to give up this struggle was heavy in the hearts of those who'd continued to wage the battle all afternoon until he could return.

The Silver Lake Fire Department rushed an emergency generator and floodlights to the scene and the battle continued. Nearly fourteen hours after Henry had first hooked the monster, the old section of the three-pound line broke for the last time. The battle was over.

Those who'd watched and those who'd fought the battle never once got a look at the fish—or whatever it was. It had never surfaced. There was too much shake and life in the catch to have been a turtle. Some of the characteristics of the fighting fish were those of a dogfish while the powerful runs and actions in deep water resembled those of an enormous catfish.

This is a true story of the "big one that got away." What it was no one really knows. This story, with its mystery creature, has become a part of northern Indiana's lake lore.

Perhaps, after all, it was a ghost fish, as elusive as the Manitou Monster or Nessie of Scotland.

❋❋❋

Merbrink Cottage
The Winona Lake House of Love

Merbrink was built for love. It still stands today, a testimony to the power of love. In earlier times it was referred to as "The Mystery House." For many years its doors were locked and its windows shuttered.

The story begins in 1878. John Cooper, an educator from New York, brought his wife and teenage daughter, Nellie, to Evansville where he became superintendent of schools. Three years passed and an illness befell Cooper, who could no longer provide for his family. His wife and daughter began taking in boarders.

One of the first lodgers was William H. Brunning, a thirty-year-old bachelor. He was a partner in his father's successful tea and spice store, and later, upon the father's death, became president and sole owner.

Perhaps Brunning fell in love with the young Nellie Cooper and she with him. It is certain that he held a deep affection for the entire Cooper family. Her husband still ill, Mrs. Cooper decided in 1901 the family should move to the popular resort community around Winona Lake. There they opened a hotel named The Homestead, which, though small, became very popular with seasonal visitors. William Brunning was a frequent visitor. One year after they moved to Winona Lake, John Cooper died. Having become attached to all the Coopers, Brunning grieved as if he were a member of the family.

Brunning decided to build an inn at the lake, the Swiss Terrace Inn, and turned the management over to Cooper's widow and daughter. That same summer Brunning purchased a lake lot. For weeks dredges and drays worked to build out and fill in the area making "Brunning's Point." Then he imported carpenters, and the house that was built for love began to take shape.

No expense was spared. It was rumored that Brunning spent over $10,000 to build Merbrink and several thousands more on the exquisite furnishings, including a beautiful piano purchased especially for Miss Nellie.

Curiosity concerning the house led the residents to wonder if it had been built as a bridal gift for Miss Nellie. It was obvious that Mr. Brunning and Miss Nellie had great affection for each other, though no engagement had been announced.

For years Mr. Brunning made regular biweekly visits to Winona Lake. On those occasions he didn't stay at Merbrink, but spent the weekend at the Swiss Terrace Inn. His appearance on those visits was that as a suitor and an admirer; each trip he'd bring a box of candy for Miss Nellie.

On Sunday afternoons it was the habit of Nellie and her mother to accompany their guest to Merbrink, where they'd spend the day together. On those occasions the villagers, making it their business to pass, could hear Miss Nellie playing the piano.

Brunning hired a local woman as housekeeper. Prior to their biweekly visits, she would make certain the house was clean and ready to receive its visitors.

The aging suitor made certain no decay crept into beautiful Merbrink. Each year it was painted anew, the piano was tuned, the water and gas pipes were checked, and any needed carpentry work done.

The grass in summer would be cut weekly. When the willow trees dropped their leaves and twigs, the yard was cleaned. And, when the waves cast driftwood over the concrete wall between the yard and the blue lake, the caretaker disposed of the debris. The snow and sleet that would blow across the wide veranda were regularly cleaned away. All was kept in readiness.

Why did they not marry? Was there some impediment? Did Mrs. Cooper object? No one knew, but the house stood beautifully groomed, obviously prepared for the love of Brunning's life.

After Nellie's mother's death, the two sweethearts were at last married. Miss Nellie was nearing sixty while her husband was twelve years her senior. The newlyweds moved to Evansville, where Brunning still maintained his spice company. But as they had in years past, every other weekend they would go to Merbrink. Their years as man and wife would be short-lived; Nellie became ill and died, and her husband followed a few years later.

The stories of these old houses are often ones of neglect and negligence, as one generation that doesn't care succeeds the one that did. Merbrink went to Brunning's nephew in California. He had no interest in the property and finally the county took it for back taxes. It was sold in 1931 to Donald White and his wife, and upon their deaths one of their two daughters, Anna Lou, became the new owner and is to this day.

Merbrink is located at 410 Administration Boulevard, Winona Lake, IN, 46590. The wraparound porch can be seen from the front.

There have been many stories written about the house. In a number of them, Anna Lou has expressed her love for Nellie and William's Merbrink. She has also stated emphatically that she feels a presence in the house, not a malevolent, but a comforting presence, which may be Nellie.

Sometimes young lovers holding hands walk three times around the house, believing this will bless their love and insure it will last like Nellie and William's—forever.

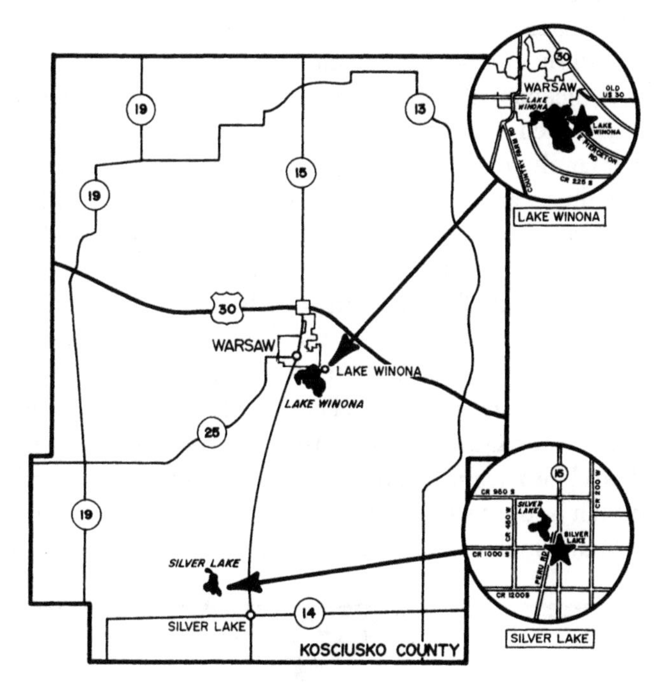

LA PORTE COUNTY

Before 1830 all of La Porte and Starke Counties were a part of the Potawatomi Nation. In 1830 all of northwestern Indiana from Elkhart County to the state line on the west was designated as St. Joseph County. Finally in 1832 an area consisting of 462 square miles was separated and a new county was created and named La Porte, meaning "the door." The area was a natural opening through the forest, which served as a gateway to the north. In 1850 twenty sections of land were taken from St. Joseph County on the east and added to La Porte County.

The area encompassing the Sauk Trail was chosen as the location for the county seat and named La Porte, for the county. La Porte city was nicknamed "The Maple City" for the maple trees lining the streets, planted as early as the 1850s. In 1829 Mrs. Benedict, a widow, and her family were the first white settlers to come to La Porte County, locating in an area just north of present-day Westville. In 1941 the United States government constructed the Kingsbury Ordnance Plant on 13,454 acres of farmland near a town laid out in 1835. The plant employed over 20,000 workers, nearly half of them being female. Testing sites, barracks, bunkers and dormitories filled the area, which was crisscrossed with railroad tracks and highways.

Pinhook was originally called New Durham and platted in 1847 and named for Durham, New York. It was supposedly nicknamed "Pinhook" for a jog in the main road, or possibly as a scornful epithet hurled at it by the neighboring village of Flood's Grove, two miles south.

Many small lakes dot the county, which is known for its beauty.

The Ghost of "J" Street Medical Clinic

One of the longest reported periods of hauntings in Indiana is in the town of La Porte at the corner of I and Tenth Streets.

For nearly one hundred years people connected with this land have reported experiencing hauntings. Perhaps these folktales reflect events that may even have been going on long before.

Originally the property where the medical clinic sits belonged to Dr. George L. Andrew, who moved to Indiana in 1845 and married a daughter of one of the founders of the city. Soon after the couple began the construction of a three-story mansion on what would become the corner of I and Tenth Street.

With a columned veranda and many rooms, the home was impressive. Five rooms were set aside above the kitchen for servants' quarters. The doctor commissioned Fredrick Law Olmsted, the designer of Central Park in New York City and a part of the Biltmore Estate, to landscape his spacious yard: Olmsted planted one of every tree native to Indiana.

When Dr. Andrew retired in 1885, the home was sold. It had gone through several owners and some remodeling, including the removal of the servants' quarters, by the time Charles Gwynne purchased the house in 1904. The Gwynnes were the first to notice the hauntings.

The story of their forty-four-year life with a live-in ghost came mainly from Mrs. Madeline Gwynne Kinney, their daughter, who was the former curator of the La Porte County Historical Museum.

One day Madeline was cleaning a closet when she heard a sound behind her like something being dropped. Turning around she saw four coins on the floor: two pennies and two nickels, dated 1876, 1877, 1867 and 1869, respectively. Where they came from was a mystery, and still is. There were no holes or cracks in the walls. From where in the world (or out of it) had these things fallen?

The ghost first made itself known by tampering with a front doorbell which had to be twisted to produce a ring. One winter night, during a particularly fierce snowstorm, the bell began to ring incessantly. Mr. Gwynne rushed down the stairs and opened the door, thinking it was someone in need of assistance, but the porch was empty. What was even more mysterious was the fact that there were no footprints in the fresh snow.

After that experience, the ghost made certain the Gwynne family didn't forget that this was its house, too. Frequently the family would hear footsteps going up and down the main staircase, and of course, no family member had been on the stairs at the time.

Before retiring, Mr. Gwynne would make certain that all doors and windows were securely locked. On a number of occasions the family would wake up to find the doors standing open and even some of the windows opened. Crashing sounds, like something being thrown or dropped, would shatter the stillness, but nothing was ever found broken.

Robert Zimmerman, La Porte's Director of Redevelopment, purchased the house from the Gwynnes in 1958. His family was the last to live in the house. They were not aware that they had purchased a house complete with a live-in ghost. Shortly after moving in they began to experience unexplained disturbances.

About 2:00 AM one night, they were awakened by a crashing sound that shook the house. Immediately afterwards there was a metallic sound that Zimmerman likened to chains clanking on sheet metal, a very tinny sound that went on for nearly thirty seconds.

They searched the house but couldn't find anything that would account for the noises. Zimmerman thought that it might have been a sonic boom and called Bunker Hill Air Force Base to see if any planes were flying in the area. He was told that because of public concerns the Air Force had curtailed flights of the B51s a month earlier.

Four months later when the daughter of the previous owner, Madeline Gwynne Kinney, asked if she could include the house in a historic home tour, she added information to Zimmerman's tale. Mrs. Kinney told the group about the "friendly ghost" that had been a part of her family when they lived there. Afterwards the new owner asked Mrs. Kinney to describe for him some of the manifestations she had experienced.

Her family, she said, had been awakened several times during the years by a loud crashing sound followed by a metallic clanking. Though she offered no explanation, Mr. Zimmerman knew what had been behind his experience, a friendly ghost of long-standing in the residence.

Zimmerman told of the incidents his family experienced with the doorbell being rung then finding no one or even footprints on the porch.

Mrs. Kinney remarked that the same thing had happened to her family on numerous occasions.

Zimmerman's daughter, Ginna, was in the rose garden picking flowers when she felt that someone was watching her. She turned around—there in the attic window she saw a woman staring down at her, with long black hair and puffed sleeves on a white blouse. When her father heard her scream that someone was in the attic, he rushed up the stairs, but found no one.

At least one incident with the ghost proved profitable. Mrs. Zimmerman, reading alone one night, heard the sound of coins falling to the floor and found on the floor six coins: a quarter, a nickel and four pennies all minted before 1900.

The family also experienced footsteps in the foyer, climbing the stairs and ending where there once was the door to the servant's quarters.

The house was sold and eventually torn down to make way for the I and

Tenth Streets La Porte Medical Clinic. But the site seems to have continued to harbor specters. Employees at the clinic reported lights turning on and off, doors opening and shutting, elevators operating on their own and moving shadows.

Whatever presence remained and materialized, or resonated its psychic energy, seemed to haunt the site, not the house. The Potawatomi would often set up temporary camps at the lake that had once been on the property. When the Indians were forced from the area they were marched past this lake. A young Indian maiden was supposed to have become ill, died and been buried on the grounds where the house was built. Perhaps in that incident lies the answer to the hauntings for those who believe in the supernatural.

❋❋❋

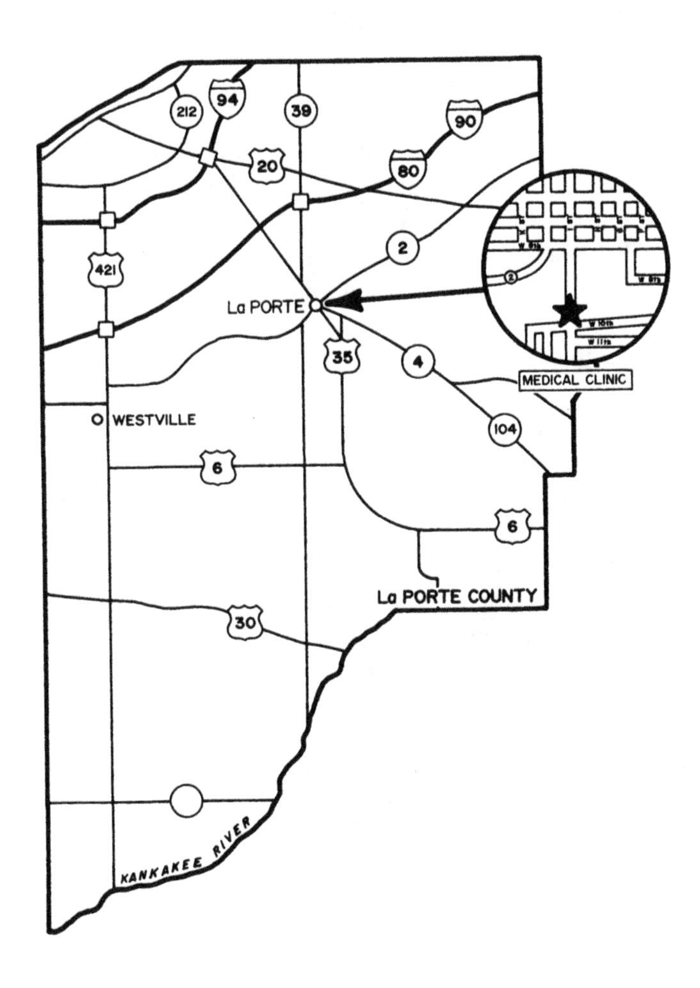

MARSHALL COUNTY

Marshall County, named for John Marshall, Chief Justice of the U.S. Supreme Court from 1801 to 1835, was organized in 1836.

The area had been the home of the Menominee tribe of Potawatomi Indians. (Potawatomi is a translation of the Ojibwe *potawatomink* meaning "People of the place of fire" or "People of the Sacred Fire," both of which refer to the role of the Potawatomi as the keepers of the sacred council fires.) Under the conditions of the 1832 Treaty of Tippecanoe River, the government purchased the land and drove the Indians westward on what became known as the Trail of Death.

Plymouth, platted in 1834 and named for Plymouth, Massachusetts, was designated as the county seat. Marshall County was one of the last counties to be inhabited in Indiana. Eventually the swampy county began to attract settlers. Farms replaced bogs, and vacationers eventually took up residence along Marshall County's beautiful lakes.

Among them are Lake of the Woods, Twin Lakes, and Lake Maxinkuckee, the second largest natural lake in Indiana. The Yellow River flows through the middle of the county toward the southwest, and crossing its southeast corner is the Tippecanoe River, which derives its name from the Potawatomi word *Ketapikonnong*, or "place of the buffalo fish."

Paukooshuck's Ghost

When the light is just right, on nights when the moon is full, travelers on Marshall County's Road 117 or 110 might glimpse the image or fleeting form of an Indian. It may be the ghost of a Potawatomi chief.

In life he was Paukooshuck, son of Potawatomi Chief Aubbeenaubbee. His story, like many good stories, is perhaps more legend than history.

When the first white settlers entered the area of Marshall County, a number of Potawatomi reservations existed as established by the treaty of 1832. The two largest were those of Chief Aubbeenaubbee and Chief Menominee.

Aubbeenaubbee's reserve, situated west of Michigan Road, extended southward into what today is northwestern Fulton County. His hunting ground extended into Marshall County.

For some time the settlers and the Indians shared in harmony the bounties of nature. Still unspoiled by the excesses of the white man, the area teemed with deer, turkeys, ducks, geese, pheasants and many fur-bearing animals.

Paukooshuck may have been born in Fulton County and most likely spent much of his boyhood following the ancient hunting trails between Fulton County's Zinks Lake and Anderson Lake, twenty miles from his father's reservation.

Leaving his father's village, he built a log cabin at Long Point, a beautiful and game-rich area on the west side of Lake Maxinkuckee, "Lake of the Boulders" in Potawatomi. He spent his days trapping beaver in the marshes around nearby Hawk or Lost Lake.

Paukooshuck's father, Aubbeenaubbee, was described as being above medium height, stoutly and compactly built. A prominent negotiator in the treaty-making decisions, his bravery was beyond reproach. He was a manly, dignified Indian, fair and just—but sometimes prone to drink.

During one of his dark and evil periods, perhaps brought on by too much whiskey, he became involved in a fight. Though he was outnumbered two to one, he fought with the ferocity born of his native instincts and learned skills that had made him a strong and admired chief. Wielding his fifteen-inch-long knife with cunning and deadly efficiency, he killed the two Indians who may have been related to him. A council was called to deliberate on his punishment, but before it was decided he compounded his offenses by committing the heinous crime of killing his wife, believing she had done some wrong to him.

The council, following an ancient custom, appointed Paukooshuck to be the avenger—to exact justice. Justice was to kill his father. When this had been done, Paukooshuck would then become chief. The deed need not be done immediately, but within a period of several months designated by the council. If he did not execute the sentence within this period, his father would go free.

When Aubbeenaubbee heard of the council's decision, he stood before his son and commanded him to execute the sentence of the council, declaring that he was ready and willing to die. Paukooshuck's respect and love would not allow him to kill his father at that time; later, the county histories report, Paukooshuck carried out the sentence on his drunken father.

It didn't take long for the white man to convince new Chief Paukooshuck to sign away the Indians' birthrights. General John Tipton, pressured by settlers who wished the final plots of land the Indians owned, ruthlessly executed a plan to seize the land and send the Indians west.

Although the Indians resisted, the Trail of Death began on September 4, 1838. The Indians were lined up and at gunpoint marched away from their tribal lands. Those who did not appear to be a threat to the soldiers were allowed to walk unrestrained. Among the group were the very old, children and babes in arms. Several were seriously ill; all were forced to march through terrible heat across northwestern Indiana.

Many died from thirst. Others succumbed to sickness. The dead were left in shallow, unprotected graves as the mourning families were forced to continue their march across Illinois.

Paukooshuck attempted to escape at every chance. As they neared the Mississippi River he made a last desperate attempt. One of the soldiers caught him and swiftly cut his throat. He was left for dead. However, the cut hadn't severed the jugular vein.

Determined to return to his home at Long Point, weak from loss of blood and the ordeal, he slowly made his way through the brush, avoiding settlements and roads for fear of being discovered and returned.

All of his friends were gone, his home on Long Point was gone, and even the wild animals seemed to have abandoned the land. The settlers had laid their claim to the land by cutting trees, plowing and planting and damming the streams. Much of the wild beauty of the area had been destroyed.

One day, drinking and wandering disheartedly, he entered Chief Winamac's village where he got into the worst fight of all. He was mortally wounded and his body was returned to Long Point.

Why does Paukooshuck's spirit appear at Long Point as some say? Why can he not break his earthly bonds? If he had been a Catholic, as Menominee was, perhaps the burden of guilt for having carried out the execution of his father keeps him from finding eternal peace.

❋❋❋

You'll Also Want to See:

The spooky House of a Thousand Candles on East Shore Road, written about by Meredith Nicholson in a well-known book of the same name, and the site of Neswaugee's Camp on 18B on a hill on the north side of the road, where within living memory sixty-four campsites have been seen at spring plowing time and some people say plumes of smoke can be seen on a moonlit night. Near Plymouth Menominee's Monument stands lonely above the settlers' cornfields that he despised on Peach Road.

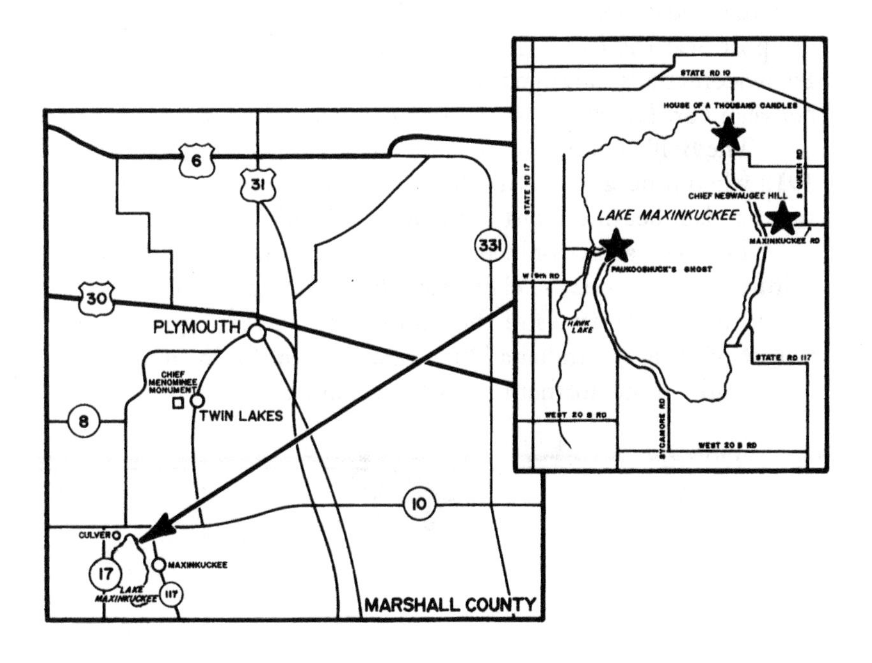

PORTER COUNTY

Established in 1835, Porter County reaches from Lake Michigan in the north to the Kankakee River in the south. The county is named for commodore David Porter, Commander of the *Essex* in the war of 1812.

Porter County contains the Indiana Dunes State Park and the Indiana Dunes National Lakeshore.

Joseph Bailly, a French-Canadian fur trader, was the first white man to settle in northwest Indiana. Arriving in 1822, he built a trading post near the Little Calumet River, where the North Sauk and Potawatomi trails converged. For ten years it was one of only two posts between Fort Dearborn (at the present site of Chicago) and Detroit.

The Bailly family occupied the forty-two-acre homestead until 1918 when it became a Catholic retreat. After passing through private hands it became a part of the national park in 1971.

The main source of income for the county had come from agriculture; however, today steel mills and Burns International Harbor are the economic mainstays of the community. Increasing numbers of tourists visiting the Indiana Dunes also account for income growth, particularly in the northern half of the county.

Child's Play

Set amidst rolling hills, rich green forests, and meandering streams, the old Timberlake Farms home exemplified Victorian style and charm.

When Timberlake Farms was put on the market in 1995, John and Linda Johnson didn't hesitate. The sheer beauty and tranquility of the surroundings captured their attention. In the middle of this perfection sat the old Ritter family home, built in the late 1800s.

The Johnsons wanted to share this beautiful setting with others. Timberlake Farms, formerly a dairy farm, then home to thoroughbred horses, is now The Inn at Aberdeen, a bed and breakfast inn at 3158 S. State Road 2 in Valparaiso.

A captivating 1878 lithograph by E. C. Barnes today hangs at the top of the winding staircase. In it a towheaded child in a white linen nightgown stands at the bottom of the stairs with a kitten in her arms and a puppy at her feet. Her saucer eyes gaze so directly they make the viewer turn away. There is more to the lithograph than meets the eye.

Shortly after the inn opened, an employee came to Johnson with a strange story. He'd been walking past the spiral staircase when he saw a little girl slowly descending.

"Well, we do have children here," Johnson said.

"Yes, but this child looked just like the little girl in the picture at the top of the stairs."

Johnson smiled and nodded. The story was interesting, but nothing more.

A little later a man and his wife commented they'd been startled when they'd encountered a little girl on the stairs. With unblinking eyes she watched them and then slowly turned and walked away. They, too, remarked that she looked like the little girl in the picture.

Mr. Johnson admits he personally has never seen the little girl, and yet he feels something is going on. Several of his guests and employees tell consistent stories of seeing the image of a little girl who eerily resembles the image in the print. Can this spectral image be only the product of overactive imaginations?

For a while the little girl seemed content to just be seen. Then guest Mary Joyce reported that she was certain the little girl had visited her room and seemed to enjoy playing pranks on her. Things would disappear and then reappear, sometimes in strange places.

One morning Joyce was dressing for an early round of golf when she found one of her socks was missing. She looked everywhere with no success.

That evening as she was preparing for bed she found the missing sock under her pillow!

Another time she couldn't find her lipstick. She'd looked everywhere, the bathroom, the dresser, her purse and then . . . there it was—in her shoe!

"It was almost like a child playing a game," she mused.

The manifestations weren't limited to sightings of the little girl or childish pranks. The Johnson's daughter Mandy and another employee, Robin Jackson, were cleaning the Aberdeen Suite when suddenly the gas fireplace turned on and off all by itself. Then they thought they heard footsteps and left as fast as they could.

The Aberdeen Suite contains the master bed and fireplace, retooled for gas, from the original house. After the girls reported what had happened Johnson had the fireplace thoroughly checked for shorts. Nothing was found to account for this newest phenomenon, nor for the fact that lights turned off and on in the basement—definitely an unnerving experience for the person left in the dark.

John and Sarah Ritter, the original owners of Timberlake, had five children. Sadly, Sarah and two of the children had died during the time they occupied the home. Is it possible that what people are experiencing is the ghost of one of the Ritter children?

Or, is there another explanation that has nothing to do with the inn, but instead the lithograph?

E. C. Barnes was a famous British artist whose career lasted only twenty-six years. But during that brief period of time he was highly praised for his realistic domestic scenes of Victorian life, especially of children. It is his lithograph that hangs at the top of the stairs.

Barnes' depictions of children are pure enchantment, so real you expect them to reach out from the canvas. Is it possible that in painting the little girl with her kitten and puppy, Barnes had captured more than her likeness?

Some primitive societies believed souls become imprisoned if one looks into a mirrored surface. The Native Americans expressed this fear of losing their souls and often refused to allow their pictures to be taken.

Has the child with the soulful eyes, who had been captured in the painting, found a way to roam free again?

❋❋❋

ST. JOSEPH COUNTY

South Bend was designated the county seat of St. Joseph County in 1830. The founder, Alexis Coquillard, originally named the area Big St. Joseph Station, but settlers called it The Bend or South Bend, because of the turn the St. Joseph River makes in the city.

The Civil War settlement of Catholic brothers and sisters brought learning and religious institutions early into the region and accelerated South Bend's and Mishawaka's economic growth. Before the Civil War, Mishawaka's Milburn Wagon Company was awarded military contracts. In 1857 Henry Milburn and Clement Studebaker became partners. By war's end Milburn and Studebaker Works were the largest businesses in the South Bend-Mishawaka area.

In 1922 South Bend's WGAZ—today's WSBTY—began broadcasting, becoming Indiana's oldest commercial station and the first commercially sponsored radio broadcast in the United States.

Today South Bend is a fast-growing center of commerce and industry, the home of the University of Notre Dame and the National Football Hall of Fame.

Osceola Poltergeist

"If I had not been witness to them I certainly would not believe such things could happen," wrote the investigating officer from the St. Joseph County sheriff's office.

Osceola, Indiana, September 1966. The family came home to discover somebody or something had entered their home on Greenlawn Avenue and left it in disarray. Furniture was toppled, and pictures, potted plants, vases and lamps were shattered. They were shocked, but for reasons best known to them they did not report the event to the police—at least not then.

The family of three—father, mother, and their nine-year-old son—had experienced other strange happenings in the past few weeks, none quite as destructive as what they'd found in their home that day. On one of these occasions the husband and wife were in bed when a key case seemed to "sail" from the dresser and fall to the floor a foot or so away.

One day the wife was in the kitchen when the iron fell from the cabinet. At first, thinking she hadn't placed it far enough back from the edge, she picked up the iron and put it back on the cabinet. No sooner had she turned around when it crashed to the floor once again.

Another incident happened when the family was watching television. They heard a sound as if something had hit the wall. When they investigated, they found a candelabra on the floor far across the room from where it normally sat on a table.

Unnerved by the experiences, the family finally decided to call the police.

Two officers from the sheriff's department came, heard the complaints, and admitted the occurrences certainly did sound like pranks, elaborate hoaxes that were also destroying property as well as frightening the family. As one of the officers walked toward the door, the second officer observed an end table moving, seemingly "following" the man and then falling over. They examined the table for wires attached to the legs but found nothing.

It was suggested that everyone leave the house. The officers thought perhaps there'd been a tremor. Calling into headquarters to inquire if there had been any reports of a possible earthquake, they ascertained there had been no earthquake tremors. Perplexed, the officers suggested some kind of a vibration had caused the table to "walk" and then fall over: a jet boom or a semi's rumbling passage nearby.

In any event the officers promised to look into the problem. As they once again began to walk out the door, they were stopped short as a picture fell from the wall. Examination proved the wire hadn't broken and the nail was still firmly in the wall. The officers looked at each other and then nodded in assent: some kind of vibration.

The two investigating officers reported all of these events in full to the sheriff.

At the "poltergeist house" disturbances continued: the breaking of dishes, vases and other small objects, as well as the strewing of clothing that had been in closets. Suspicious eyes were quite naturally cast on the nine-year-old boy in the household; he denied involvement.

At first Sheriff Locks treated the disturbances seriously. At the South Bend library he pored over books about poltergeists and even magic.

Many people in the community were speculating and some were snickering. But the sheriff continued his search for an answer, no matter how bizarre that answer might be.

He'd received reports of strange lights in the skies over St. Joseph County. He wondered if there could be any connection between the "poltergeist" activities and these reports.

In his search of an answer, he turned to the University of Notre Dame. A team of men from the psychology, chemistry and physics departments visited the home. They examined everything from the foundation to the plumbing and heating systems, and talked to the members of the family and neighbors.

They believed this was a many-sided problem. Still, they couldn't say what was causing the anomalies, such as a small evergreen beside the front door bending over, touching the ground and then popping back into place. There wasn't any wind activity when this occurred. What in the world (or out of it) was the explanation?

The Notre Dame team on October 12, 1966 stated in an interview, "We have found no logical explanation for what has happened in this house."

Finally the activity stopped just as mysteriously as it had begun.

On October 14, 1966 the sheriff called a press conference in his South Bend office. In that news conference the sheriff stated that all of the things that had happened in the house were caused by the actions of a juvenile and the case was closed. He refused to answer any further questions or to discuss the incident ever again.

The activities had ceased. The family was satisfied. But others, hearing the case was closed, continued to ask, "How?" "Who?" "Why?"

❋ ❋ ❋

WHITLEY COUNTY

Organized in 1838, Whitley County was named for Colonel William Whitley, killed at the Battle of the Thames, Canada, 1813, during the War of 1812.

As a result of the treaties of 1826 and 1828 the county's first land sales began in 1833 and lasted until 1848. Both the Miami and the Potawatomi claimed land in this territory. They actually established only one settlement, Seek's Village.

Little Turtle, the great Miami, was born about five miles east of Columbia City, the county seat.

The Wabash and Erie Canal, which opened from Fort Wayne to Huntington in 1835, helped develop the southeastern corner of the county.

Agriculture was the county's main occupation. From 1900 through the 1920s, Whitley County competed with Noble County in growing onions. Collins, northeast of Columbia City, claimed to be the Onion Capital of the nation.

The northern part of the county is noted for its picturesque lakes. In the tri-lakes region around Cedar, Round and Shriner lakes resorts flourished during the 1920s.

Churubusco united the twin towns of Union and Franklin, which joined as a single town in order to gain a post office. Taking its name from the 1847 Battle of Churubusco, a decisive American victory during the Mexican War, today the town is famous as the site of a giant monster hunt.

Oscar, the Beast of "Busco"

The Indian chief Little Turtle lived in the Churubusco area. In 1847 the establishment of a post office made Churubusco an official town. But for the first one hundred years of its existence "Busco" was virtually unknown. Then Oscar came to town.

Oscar was a giant turtle, bigger than Godzilla. One man's obsession to find this giant turtle ended just like the fabled race with the hare—the turtle won.

The story begins in July 1948. Two friends from Churubusco, Ora Blue and Charley Wilson, decided to go fishing in Fulk Lake on Gale Harris' property and came away with the darndest "fish" story anyone had ever heard—not really about a fish that got away, but rather a GIANT TURTLE!

The two fishermen weren't the only ones who saw a giant turtle that day. Gale Harris and his minister were patching Harris' roof. From that vantage point, they could see the lake. And what they said they saw was a huge turtle in nearby Fulk Lake. Later the turtle was named Oscar, for the original owner of the land, Oscar Fulk.

Most turtles from this area weighed ten or twelve pounds. Harris and the minister said this one was five feet wide and six feet long. Its shell was so large you could set out dinner for eight on his back. He had a mouth so large he could eat a soccer ball.

This wasn't the first time a large turtle had been sighted in Fulk Lake. Oscar Fulk claimed to have spotted a giant turtle in 1898, with another sighting in 1914.

During the first days of March 1949, Harris saw the turtle again. Some of the people in Churubusco weren't sure about Harris' story; many others simply ridiculed him. A group of townspeople jokingly suggested he try to capture it. He determined to do just that.

Editors across the nation snapped up the story, splashing it in the headlines from coast to coast, and Churubusco had its own Loch Ness Monster. Radio and newspapers across the nation fell in love with the tale and even some European papers picked up the story.

According to one newspaper report, Oscar was nearly caught on the first day of Harris' efforts. Harris had constructed a trap of stakes and chicken wire in about ten feet of water. The unwitting turtle had managed to become penned in the primitive trap. But you don't catch a legend that easily. Oscar flexed some muscle and propelled himself out of the trap.

Harris then invented a sort of "periscope" that allowed him to peer into the murky lake water, hoping to get a glimpse of Oscar. Next he obtained a full diving suit and talked one of his friends into putting it on to seek out Oscar on the lake bottom. Unfortunately, the helmet leaked and the diver nearly drowned.

Five days after the hunt began, nearly two hundred people began to converge on Harris' farm to watch the search. Planes flew overhead, circling the lake hoping for a glimpse of the turtle.

Someone brought a female sea turtle to lure Oscar—that didn't work either. By May public interest was finally waning, but not Harris'. He decided to use dynamite to "shock" Oscar to the surface. This only succeeded in making a big splash.

Finally, in one last-ditch effort, Harris took his tractor to the lake and hooked up a sump pump to pump the water out of that seven-acre lake so Oscar would have no place to hide.

Public interest was revived and the crowds returned. During the process Harris burned 2,000 gallons of gas as he pumped water day and night. The seven-acre lake had been reduced to one.

Thousands of people, including senators and celebrities, gathered each weekend hoping to see the world-famous turtle. On October 13 two hundred people had gathered around the lake. Harris decided to try to lure the turtle out of hiding by using a duck for bait. Suddenly, before the astonished eyes of the onlookers, Oscar propelled himself out of the water, grabbed the duck, and disappeared.

Finally the pump wore out and the trackor broke down. A crane was brought in to dredge the last acre of lake. But by December 1949 there still was enough water to hide Oscar.

Harris suffered an appendicitis attack and was hospitalized. The search had to be suspended. The weather turned nasty. By the time Harris was released from the hospital the lake had refilled with rainwater. Disheartened, he realized the search was over. The following year the farm was sold, giant turtle and all.

No one has searched for Oscar since 1949. And there have been no reported sightings. But then, who really wants to find Oscar? The legend is a lot more fun than the real turtle ever would have been.

✻✻✻

Things go Bump in a Grand Manor

Hazelcot Castle

The mystical fairytale castle, Hazelcot, was left abandoned, forlorn and under siege. No one was left to love and care for it—at least no one in this world. Protected only by its bleak joyless appearance, the silent house stood for years with dark, fathomless windows, eyes watching. But it had not always been so.

Dr. Eli Pierce and his family had a comfortable life in Albany, New York. A successful medical practice as well as such other business ventures as partnerships in pottery manufacturing and a horse-powered ferry on the Hudson made him "well-to-do." Dr. Pierce's wife, Sarah, had just come into a fortune left her by an elderly maiden aunt in whose spacious home the family had lived. They then decided to "go west."

Dr. Pierce's brother had recently moved to Fort Wayne, Indiana, and extolled the opportunities available in this old town in the northern part of the state. His wife was more than agreeable to moving. With two young sons, she'd become increasingly concerned about the corrupting influence of the river men's uncouth world in the Hudson riverboat settlement.

Dr. Pierce hired a land agent to act on his behalf. Soon the Pierces received word they now owned over five hundred acres in northeastern Indiana, about fourteen miles west of Fort Wayne in Whitley County.

Through the years their holdings would increase to over eighteen thousand acres.

Dr. Pierce sold his practice and Sarah's aunt's home but retained his business interests, then bade good-bye to New York.

The canal boats were loaded with their belongings, the necessities for erecting a sawmill, a carpenter to run the sawmill and build the house, and the Pierce family. With the money from the sales and Sarah's inheritance safely secreted in the hidden till box of one of the many trunks, they began the long, arduous journey.

Their new home in Whitley County would be built among a dense hazel grove at the foot of rolling hills. The grove was the inspiration for the name of the estate—Hazelcot (*cot* from the Old English word for shelter).

Dr. Pierce set up his sawmill in a grove of black walnut trees and provided the lumber for his own house. Since Sarah was used to a style of elegant living (she told visitors she was descended from English gentry) she wished the home built in the English Manor House style.

It was 1835 when the family moved into the new home, Sarah was pleased. Hazelcot was indeed a castle, constructed of black walnut with wide porches, huge columns and a grand interior consisting of twenty-six rooms, fourteen fireplaces, a spacious dining hall and doublewide staircases at each end of the home.

Crowning its architectural structure was the huge library that Sarah filled with leather-bound volumes her family had brought from England.

Clearly Sarah was impressed with "position." Almost immediately she began planning elegant dinners, inviting those whom she felt to be influential—the "right people." Dr. Pierce had invited the county treasurer to one of these dinners. Later, in recounting the evening, the treasurer spoke of a conversation he had with the hostess. Mrs. Pierce had asked him if his treasurer's position was one of much dignity and when the unassuming official replied, "None at all,"

Sarah immediately turned her full attention to other guests.

Dr. Pierce began practicing medicine again while maintaining lucrative partnerships, increasing his fortune. The land holdings around Hazelcot grew to more than 18,000 acres.

Sarah continued to revel in her manor house for five more years, then died. Dr. Pierce remained in the house. Their children matured, married and left the castle. However, the oldest son, his wife, Mary Ann, and their children remained to assist Dr. Pierce in running his vast estate and business interests.

On Easter Sunday, 1874, Dr. Pierce died. On that day the aged doctor, intent on attending Easter services at Fort Wayne's Trinity church, had left Hazelcot on foot heading toward Arcola. There he would board a train and ride the ten miles to Fort Wayne. His body was found along the roadside about half way between Hazelcot and the railroad station. He had suffered a heart attack.

The doctor's son continued to care for Hazelcot, leaving the house only after his own wife's death. None of the family wanted Hazelcot after Pierce's son's death. According to the stories surrounding the castle, not one of them ever returned to Hazelcot for anything.

Hazelcot sat intact and unoccupied, complete with furniture, crystal chandeliers, Sarah's books, even Dr. Eli's hat and medical bag. No longer called Hazelcot, the house soon became known as the Haunted House.

A group of three lads decided to enter the abandoned house one moonlit night to see if the house, as reported, was haunted. Quietly they ascended the wide, debris-littered stairs. Slowly and uneasily they pushed the door open. The tomblike quiet was broken by the sound of scurrying mice.

They turned the knob of another door, the one opening to the library. There, in the middle of the room, sat a woman with long hair touching the floor, a book in her hand. The boys turned and ran out of the house.

No one believed the ghost story they told over the next few days. Perhaps they'd seen an escaped inmate from a Fort Wayne institution? She would have had to wander through the countryside for miles until she reached Hazelcot, where she rested for a while, then left.

An elderly man working at a riding stable heard the boys' story and could vouch that the house was really haunted. He said he'd worked for Dr. Pierce's family. His room was at the top of the back stairs. He always kept his lantern lit when he went to bed. Many nights he'd wake up to feel a hand on his throat. He'd jump out of his bed, grab the lantern and down the steps he'd go. "I wouldn't go back to that room that night. Oh, it was a terrible place. No doubt about it."

Time passed and fear of the haunted house gave way to practicality. The informal neighborhood dismantling of the structure began, as the need for wood to build houses and barns took precedence over legal quibbling.

The barns were the first to go. Then the castle was invaded. Woodwork was pried loose, black walnut doors removed. Piece by piece the house was dissected, stripped, and disemboweled.

In 1893 the ruins were cleared away. All the land was sold by proxy. All that's left buried in the tangle of hazel brush are a few foundation bricks.

Historians in the area believe many older homes still standing today have walnut woodwork and other appointments from Hazelcot. In 1971 the Whitley County Historical Society erected a marker to commemorate Hazelcot Castle. The marker is on the east side of Johnson Road and north of the intersection of De La Balme Road and Johnson Road. Vandals have pried off the metal plaque but the base remains solid.

Fear of the "haunted" house gave way to practicality and it was dismantled in 1893. When the winter winds chill the air, who can say what will be seen in the hazel grove.

Drawing by Allen White

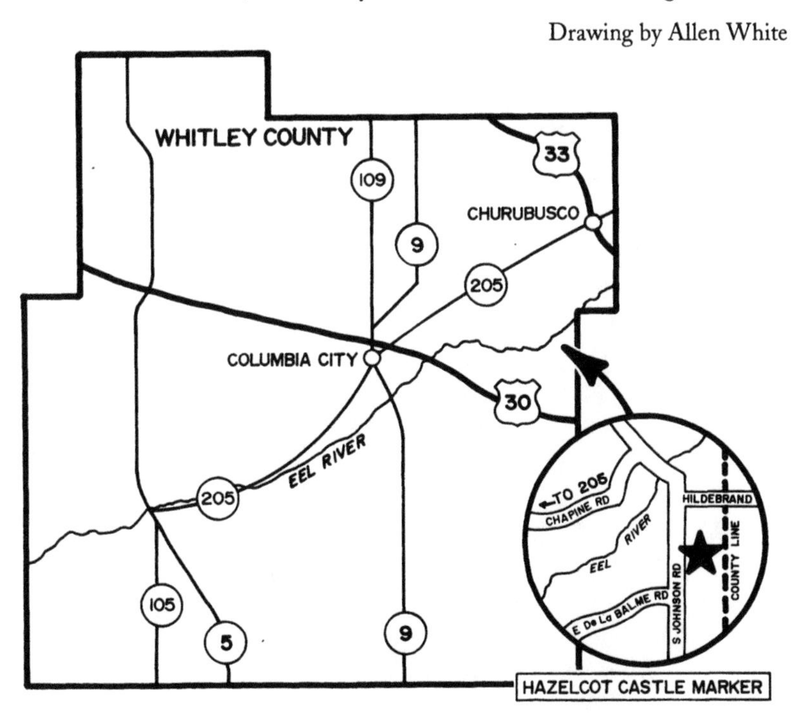

Central Indiana

CLAY COUNTY

Clay County, organized in 1825, was named for Henry Clay, Kentucky orator and statesman. In the 1809 Treaty of Fort Wayne, the Miami, Delaware and the Eel River Indians ceded the land to the United States. The Indians referred to this part of Indiana as the "famous hunting ground," and it was reputed to be the best territory in the Indiana Territory. The county is shaped by ten right angles and was formed from parts of Vigo, Sullivan, Putnam and Owen Counties.

Historically coal and clay have been important to the county's economy. The clay was the basis for a number of pottery and brick factories. Clay City evolved because of its location on the Cincinnati and Terre Haute Railway. The Clay City Pottery Company, started by Welshman Beryl Griffith, began operation in 1885 and is still owned and operated by the same family. Coal continues to be mined in the county.

Brazil has been the county seat since 1877, when the courthouse records were secretly removed from Bowling Green, the first county seat, and transported to the newly built courthouse at Brazil. Platted in 1844, the town is supposed to have received its name from a local citizen who happened to be reading news about Brazil, South America at the time. The town developed into a coal-shipping center in the 1850s. Among Brazil's coal drillers was John Cleveland Hoffa, whose son, James R. Hoffa, born in Brazil in 1913, rose through the union ranks to lead the International Brotherhood of Teamsters from 1957 to 1971. The Hoffa family lived in Brazil until 1922.

The One-Hundred Steps Cemetery

The One-Hundred Steps Cemetery near Brazil is located on CR 675, just west of the 340 jog on US 40. Climbing the stairs on the side of the grassy hill, surrounded by old gravestones dating back to the 1860s can raise one's heart rate, but knowing what awaits at the top of the stairs will also add to the pounding of a hiker's heart.

Most of the One-Hundred Steps Cemetery stories deal with counting the number of steps both going up and down and getting the same number both times. Few people, if any, have been able to accomplish this feat. The most logical reason for this is that the steps are cracked, broken and often buried under patches of grass.

Other than a physical and counting exercise, what would be the purpose in counting these steps and what are the consequences?

Folklore in the area suggests that if a climber dares to venture to the cemetery at midnight and hikes to the top of the hill counting the steps—and, perhaps, panting a little—when he reaches the top that person will see how he will die.

After reaching the top, old-timers say, you must turn toward the open field and be prepared for what will happen next. Approaching in the moonlight will be the ghost of the first cemetery's undertaker. Without a word he will reveal to the climber a vision of that person's own death. Then he will disappear.

The hiker must proceed down the steps, counting once more. If he or she doesn't get the same number as before, the vision will come true.

If one dares try to reach the top or return to level ground by not using the steps, he or she will be pushed to the ground by a phantom hand which will leave a red imprint on the individual's back for several days, so those in the neighborhood can see the mark of the Devil.

No one knows the consequences of this encounter, but it certainly must be so horrible no one wants to take the chance.

⁂

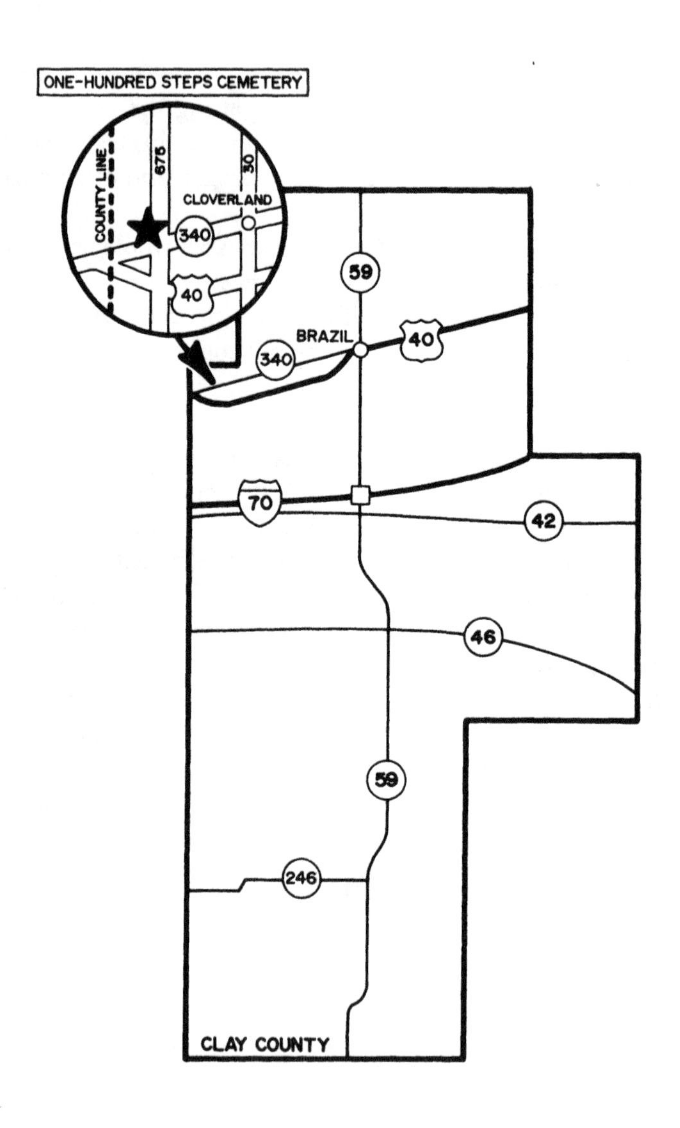
ONE-HUNDRED STEPS CEMETERY
COUNTY LINE
675
30
CLOVERLAND
340
40
59
BRAZIL
340
40
70
42
46
59
246
CLAY COUNTY

FOUNTAIN COUNTY

Created in 1826, Fountain County was formed from portions of Montgomery and Wabash Counties and was named for Major James Fountain, who had been killed near Fort Wayne in the Battle of Maumee in 1790.

The county seat, Covington, which might have been named for Covington, Virginia, and the county's largest city, Attica, both border the Maumee River. Covington was platted in 1828 by Isaac Coleman, a Virginian who settled there in 1826.

About seven miles north of Covington on the Wabash River is the town of Fountain. Fountain, originally a trading-post town, was laid out as Portland in 1828. Between 1846 and 1875 Fountain participated in trade on the Wabash and Erie Canal along a 376-mile stretch through Indiana from Fort Wayne to Evansville. A towpath still follows the riverbank on the west side of town.

George Hollingsworth, who operated a ferry across the Wabash, laid out Attica in 1825. In the early years Attica competed with Covington for trade on the Wabash and Erie Canal, which had been opened to Attica in 1847. With the collapse of the canal system in 1881, the Wabash Railroad opened a branch line from Attica to Covington using the canal's towpath.

In 1807 Tecumseh and his brother the Prophet represented the Shawnee at a council meeting with the Kickapoo, Potawatomi, Miami and Winnebago Indians held under a giant oak tree in what today is Attica. In 1866 the Council Oak was cut down. A marker on the south wall of the Attica City Hall identifies the spot.

Veedersburg, the county's second largest town, was laid out in 1871 by Peter S. Veeder and others. Veedersburg was an early manufacturing center for bricks.

Chambermaid Haunts Hotel
Attica, Indiana

The Attica Hotel has had more than its share of bad luck through the years. The site of the present hostelry first housed the two-story Revere House built in 1837, which burned to the ground around 1844. The following year the rebuilt hotel opened at 126 N. Perry Street in Attica and was renamed the Attica Hotel.

It soon became known as "the traveling man's home away from home," the finest hotel in the Midwest, with its second story decorated with ornate New Orleans-style ironwork and featuring gracious hospitality. Many of the Wabash and Erie canal workers made the hotel their home during the construction of the canal segment that went through Attica.

Bad luck literally hit the second hotel when a devastating tornado in 1886 destroyed the north wall. After that part of the building was rebuilt, a fire in 1908 destroyed the entire north wing.

Though the hotel had its troubles, it continued to be a stylish hostelry. For forty years beginning in 1920 it boasted what was considered to be the best prime rib restaurant in the Midwest. People going to the Warren County spa, Mudlavia, approximately eight miles from Attica, would spend the night in the hotel primarily to enjoy the prime ribs.

The Attica Hotel hosted such celebrity guests as Bette Davis, Bing Crosby, Al Jolson, and Alfonso "Al" Capone, who wished to "take the waters," or rest.

But the bad luck jinx struck again in the 1950s. Vida Foxworthy, a chambermaid at the hotel, was murdered while cleaning one of the rooms. Her murderer was never apprehended.

Soon after the murder, several guests reported strange occurrences. They heard footsteps in the hallway when no one was there. The owner at the time believed her dog, Maggie, who had been fond of Vida, could see her apparition. At times Maggie would wag her tail and lift her head in happy expectation of a pat from her friend.

Vida is a playful ghost. A pool player was sighting his shot. He reported that when he was ready to make it, she nudged the pool stick; he missed the shot and lost the game.

Vida doesn't restrict her playfulness to just dogs and pool players. One day a female advertising representative sitting in the lobby was pleasantly surprised when someone began to rub her neck. Smiling, she turned her head to see who the individual was and got the shock of her life. No one was near her!

Usually haunted rooms have cold spots. Here's a switch: During the winter of 1993 when the hotel's heating system stopped operating, the room in which the murder occurred was twenty degrees warmer than any other room in the hotel. Even when hotel rooms were closed for renovation and redecoration, footsteps continued to be heard in the upstairs hallway.

Today, the Attica Hotel operates as a restaurant serving evening meals only.

❋❋❋

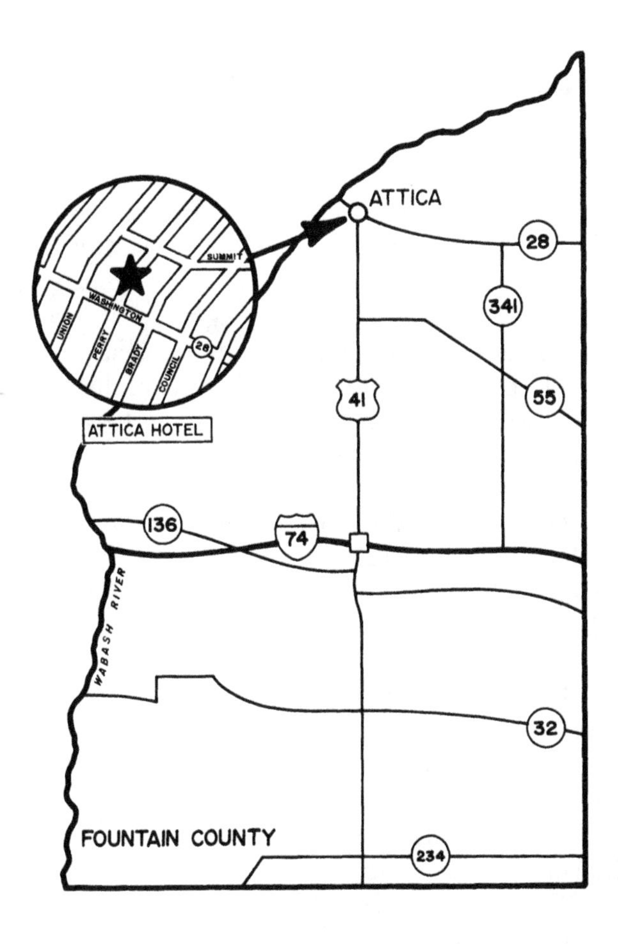

FRANKLIN COUNTY

Franklin, Indiana's seventh county, was formed from portions of Dearborn, Fayette and Union Counties in 1811 and named for the Revolutionary War statesman Benjamin Franklin.

Brookville, the county seat, was founded in 1808 by Amos Butler and Jesse Thomas and became the seat of government in 1811. Construction of the Whitewater Canal, beginning at Brookville in 1836, and the great German migration into the Whitewater Valley in the 1830s added to the economic development of the community.

Brookville was the home of Indiana governors. Lew Wallace, the author of *Ben Hur*, was born in Brookville in 1827. His father, David Wallace, was governor of Indiana from 1837 to 1840. Another Indiana governor (1860-1861), Abram Hammond, also lived in Brookville as a boy in the "Old Yellow Tavern," now the site of the county jail. Governor James B. Ray, who served from 1825 to 1831, also had lived in Brookville.

Laurel, platted in 1836, prospered especially after 1843 when the Whitewater Canal reached the town from Brookville. It became a major shipping point and a center of limestone quarrying. After the canal era, the town languished.

Metamora, another important canal town, was platted in 1838. Mrs. John A. Matson is credited with naming the town Metamora after an Indian princess character in a popular contemporary play in New York. The town's prosperity fell with the ending of the Whitewater Canal's importance. However, in the 1940s the town's economics improved when local and state efforts began to restore and preserve the canal and surviving buildings. Today it is recognized as the Whitewater Canal State Historic Site, and has become a popular tourist attraction. Many of the original buildings have been preserved, including the Van Camp Drug Store, built in 1853 by the Van Camp family. An explosion in 1870 destroyed much of the building and killed four family members, including Mrs. Van Camp and one of her sons. Another son, Gilbert, later moved to Indianapolis and founded the Van Camp canning company.

Oldenburg is another interesting Franklin County community that has preserved its religious, cultural and architectural heritage. Originally settled by Irish in 1817, it was platted in 1837 by German speculators who named it for the German province of Oldenburg. The town is known as the "Village of Spires" because of the number of churches and religious institutions.

The White Hall Tavern

In 1837 Laurel, Indiana, just eight miles northwest of the old canal town of Metamora, was a booming hub of activity, as canal workers, their families and travelers crowded the streets.

Squire Clements' White Hall Tavern, located at the corner of Baltimore and Franklin Streets, was an important and very busy hotel during the canal heyday and for several years afterwards. Its stone steps led down to the boat landing at the canal basin.

Squire Clements was a well liked, robust, jovial man known for his hospitality. Even the somewhat rowdy Irish boatmen respected him—though he refused to sell liquor.

One day a canal packet tied up at the boat landing for what was to be an overnight stay for the passengers. However, the next day one of them had to be left behind—a young pregnant wife on her way out west to meet her husband.

During the early morning hours she went into labor. Mrs. Clements attended to the young woman. Before the packet left the dock, Clements sent a message to the captain telling him to find the woman's husband and notify him that she had given birth and was too weak to travel.

It became apparent to Mrs. Clements that both the mother, already weakened by her trip, and the babe were very feeble.

Throughout the next few days, the Clements and patrons heard the young mother trying to soothe her poor babe's crying. One night around midnight a renewed fit of crying awakened the Clements. Listening they heard the mother gently trying to hush the child. After a while they realized the crying and the mother's attempts to quiet the babe were gradually weakening. Then there was silence. The rest of the night they heard nothing more from babe or mother.

The next morning Mrs. Clements discovered both were dead, the child cradled in the arms of its mother. The innkeeper and his wife saw to it that both were properly buried with a small stone bearing the mother's name and one carved merely "baby." Waiting and hoping that her husband would come for them, the young mother had declined to name the baby until its father arrived.

Long after the canals ceased to be used, the White Hall Tavern continued to provide room and board to travelers. Many of its guests reported hearing the sounds of a baby crying and a woman's gentle soothing voice—and there was, of course, no baby staying at the inn. Though the crying would be heard at various times of the day and night, the sounds were reportedly heard most frequently around midnight.

For nearly 160 years the White Hall Tavern has existed as a silent monument to Indiana's canal era. Today the tavern sits forlorn and empty. There's no one to hear the baby crying and the mother's voice gently soothing the child, only the wind.

White Hall Tavern sits near the site of the vanished Wabash and Erie canal.

Photo by Don Dunaway

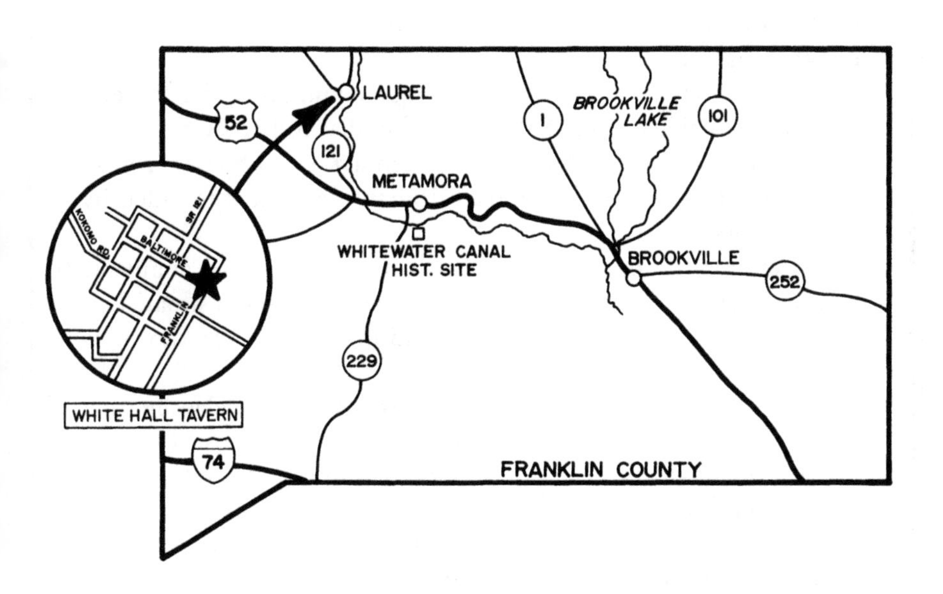
LAUREL
52
BROOKVILLE
LAKE
1
101
121
METAMORA
WHITEWATER CANAL
HIST. SITE
BROOKVILLE
252
229
KOKOMO RD.
SR 121
BALTIMORE
FRANKLIN
WHITE HALL TAVERN
74
FRANKLIN COUNTY

HAMILTON COUNTY

Organized in 1823 and named for American statesman Alexander Hamilton, this county was mainly agricultural. Although it still has thousands of acres of farmland, it is fast becoming an affluent residential area for people working in Indianapolis. It is one of the fastest-growing counties in the U.S. today.

The remains of an early and unique community, the Roberts settlement established in 1838, can be found at Roberts Chapel and Cemetery. The settlement, comprised of individuals who were a mixture of white, black and Cherokee Indian blood, was founded by Hanzel Roberts.

Perhaps the most well known historic site in the county is Conner Prairie Pioneer Settlement, an open air museum situated on the site of William Conner's homestead in an area once known as Horseshoe Prairie.

Conner (1777–1855) acquired the land from the Delaware tribe in 1802 and constructed a log cabin and fur trading post. He later married Mekinges, the daughter of the Delaware Chief Anderson, but in 1820 the Indian wife and her children went west with the rest of the tribe. That same year Conner married Elizabeth Chapman and constructed the area's first brick home.

The county seat, Noblesville, was surveyed and platted by William Conner and Josiah F. Polk in 1823. Legend has it that Polk named the settlement for his fiancée, Lavinia Noble, but it may have been called Noblesville to honor United States senator James Noble.

In 1925 the Hamilton County Courthouse in Noblesville gained national attention as the site of the D. C. Stephenson trial. The Grand Dragon of Indiana's Ku Klux Klan was convicted of second-degree murder in the death of Madge Oberholtzer, a statehouse secretary, and given a life sentence, thus breaking the throttle hold the Klan had on the state of Indiana.

The Haunting of Eck House

The new house Leonard Eck built for his wife, Irene, during the Depression was an elegant country estate that was the envy of its neighbors. The house had a huge living room with a fireplace, a dining room, a kitchen, three bedrooms, a family or playroom, a coal furnace in the basement and a laundry room where Irene could wash and in bad weather hang the clothes to dry. Certainly it was a fine replacement for the old log house where the Ecks had formerly lived.

Even as a child Toni Boone remembered her family driving past the impressive Eck house and telling herself, "Someday that will be my house." After Toni had married, she told her mother about her dream of owning the Eck house. Her mother reminded her it would be years before the Eck house would be on the market. Leonard had died several years earlier and Irene continued to live alone. In 1983, when Irene was in her eighties, her sons found her dead. The sons could not reach an agreement on what to do with the house.

For two years, as the house sat vacant, Toni often drove by just to look at her dream. Because the house had not been put on the market and no one was living in it or evidently caring for it, she feared that eventually it would be vandalized.

When a water pipe in the kitchen broke during a storm, extensive damage was done throughout the house, with hardwood dining room floors buckling and kitchen linoleum cracking and crumbling. Rather than spend the money to fix the house, the Eck family put it on the market as a fixer-upper.

Toni and her husband, Larry, a doctor in Cicero, were the excited new owners of the Eck house. They knew it would take effort to correct the damage caused during the storm, but it was worth every dollar.

The house soon began to come alive. Walls were painted and the hardwood floors refinished. Everything was going quite well until Toni and her husband began working in the kitchen.

There seemed to be something unseen hampering every move. The work of cleaning off old scaling and chipping paint was slow, tedious and irritating. Much of it even defied paint remover. The couple finally had to use a sander on the walls.

When new cabinets were ordered, none of the cabinets fit. When Toni's husband put down plywood sub-flooring, tiles popped up. He resealed them. The next day they came loose again. Changing the adhesive made no difference. Day after day troubles occurred. Toni and Larry were baffled.

One day a psychic friend came by to see the house. Looking in the direction of the fireplace, she turned back to Toni and said, "I don't want to worry or frighten you but I see a sturdily-built little man, his head just to the mantel shelf, and he's smoking a pipe that curves down."

"That's Leonard!" Toni shouted. "He was so short. He always smoked that bulldog-type pipe with the bent-down stem." The pipe had been as much a part of Leonard's body as his nose or ears. He even talked with it resting in the corner of his mouth.

"Leonard is a happy spirit, but not always," the psychic went on. "He's been responsible for all of the troubles you've been experiencing especially in the kitchen. He didn't want any changes made in the house. Most of all, he feared major alterations—he was afraid you'd start knocking out walls!"

The psychic continued. "He didn't object to the papering and painting after he saw it was being done to perfection. Changes and confusions get spirits upset. Sometimes they do things like stealing tools from workmen and then putting them back after a long search or they make their footsteps heard or get noisy, hoping to scare away the occupants. Irene, though, is happy you're here."

After that day there were no more disturbances. Then one spring day Toni began trimming the dead brush out of a long-neglected spirea bush. As she worked she wondered if she was doing it correctly when the pruners seemed to be yanked out of her hands and dropped to the ground. "I guess I'm through, right, Leonard?"

The Eck House is at 2811 Cumberland Road in Cicero.

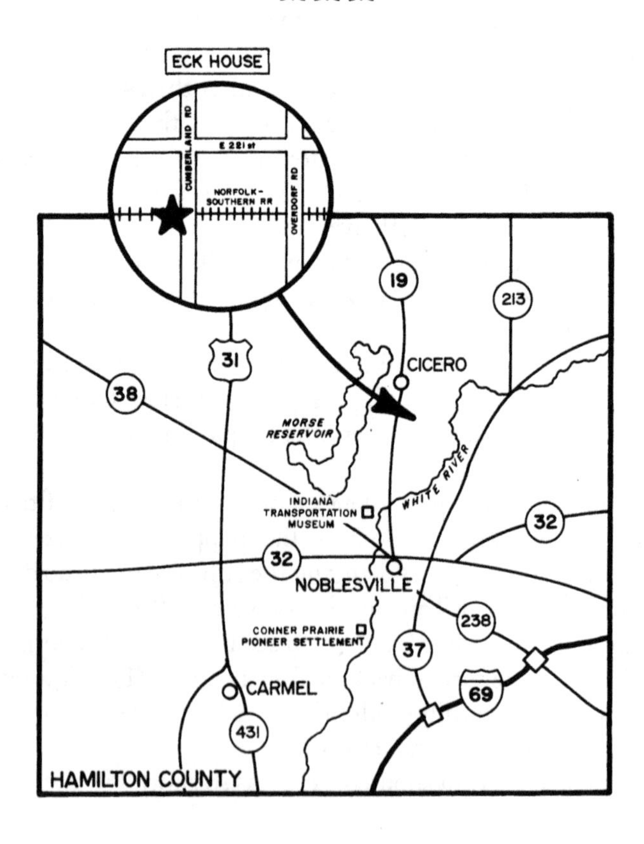

HANCOCK COUNTY

Named for the first signer of the Declaration of Independence, John Hancock, the county was organized January 1827. Hancock remains principally an agricultural county, though in the last ten years it has seen the growth of suburban sprawl.

Greenfield, the county seat, was located in the center of the county along the National Road. The gas boom of the 1890s boosted the local economy with an increase in businesses, primarily glass companies.

Greenfield is synonymous with Hoosier poet James Whitcomb Riley (1849–1916) whose family home located at 250 West Main (US 40) is operated as a museum and open to the public. Situated at the courthouse's north entrance off US 40 (Main St.) is a life-sized statue of Riley dedicated in 1918. The inscription on the granite pedestal reads "James Whitcomb Riley/Erected by American School Children."

A marker on E. Main near the entrance to Riley Park commemorates Greenfield as the birthplace of the Democratic Party Rooster, which first came to prominence in the 1840 presidential campaign when a local man, Joseph Chapman, invented the rooster insignia, which was later replaced by the donkey.

The Plantation Club's Hoodlums and Haunts

Hooligans, hoodlums, hooch and haunts: the Plantation Club had them all. The club was a 1920s roadhouse, speakeasy, casino and possibly safe house for such gangsters as Al Capone and John Dillinger.

To escape the jurisdiction of Indianapolis authorities, the McCordsville establishment was built just past the county line on an empty stretch of State Road 36.

Local lore insists that the FBI raided the club on a weekly basis. During one of these raids, Dillinger was chased out the door and across the road, making his getaway by jumping aboard a passing freight train.

During the 1920s and 1930s dice were tossed at the Plantation Club, liquor ran freely, and ladies of the night entertained in the row of cabins located behind the club. It's believed that at least two murders were committed at the club during its colorful existence.

The owner of the club made certain his "girls" were dressed in the finest and most attractive gowns. One night a patron took a shine to one of the "ladies," a willowy, long legged blond in a clinging blue gown. They danced and drank and laughed and then, arm in arm, they left the crowded club as she led him to one of the cabins where they could be alone. After a period of time they emerged from the cabin. An argument erupted. The man pulled a gun and shot the lady in blue.

The cabins are long gone, but a number of area residents claim they still see the "lady in blue" wandering the property from time to time.

For the second murder, local lore has it that a recently married young woman had been hired to work in the Plantation cloakroom. The knowledge of the illicit activities that went on in the cabins behind the club led the husband's imagination to run wild.

Sounds of laughter and partying at the club were silenced by the piercing screams of the woman as her husband shot her, continuing to squeeze the trigger until the gun was empty. When it was over, her lifeless, bullet-riddled body lay in a pool of blood on the cloakroom floor.

Stories grew as the years passed that the murdered woman still frequents the cloakroom—a ghostly attendant waiting to take coats.

The Plantation as it once was no longer exists. For many years it was the Casio's Restaurant. It retained much of the club's ambience, including the cloakroom and the steel-lined, bulletproof cashier's room, which looked as it had in the 1920s and 1930s when the cashier, with machine gun close at hand, sat on his stool watching the activity in the casino. If there was trouble, the cashier could retreat behind the bulletproof panels, grab the cash box and make his getaway through a trapdoor in the floor and into a quarter-mile tunnel leading into the woods on the edge of the property. Many years ago the tunnel was filled in and the entrance bricked up, but the memories evoked wonder for dinner guests over the years.

Some of the Casio's employees reported feeling as if someone was watching them as they passed the cloakroom. Though the cabins were no longer on the premises, a few of the employees reported seeing the "lady in blue" wandering the grounds. These tales of ghosts haunting the premises are more than legend to many. Some employees even refused to be alone in the restaurant after dark.

❋ ❋ ❋

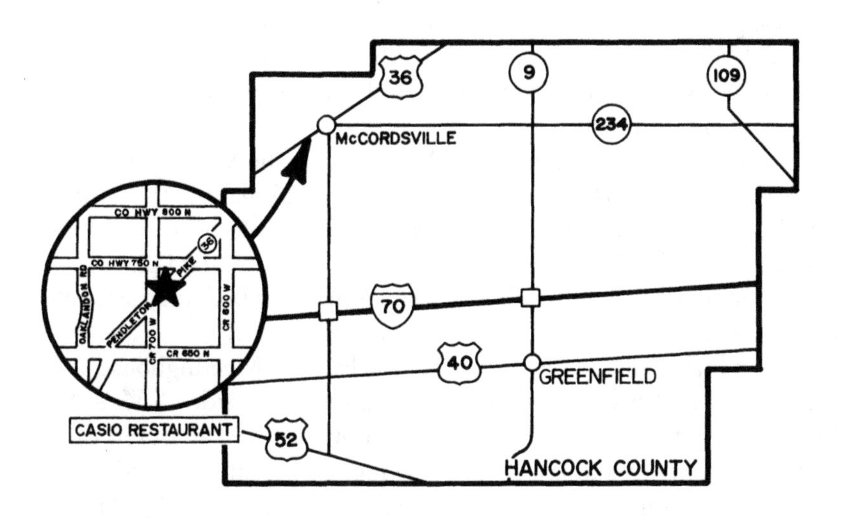

HENDRICKS COUNTY

Created in 1823, Hendricks County was named for William Hendricks, governor of Indiana at the time the county was established.

Danville, the county seat, was laid out in 1824. Judge William Wick presumably named the county seat in honor of his brother, Daniel Wick. During the period that he served as governor, 1891 to 1893, Ira J. Chase (1834–1895) lived in Danville and commuted daily to Indianapolis by train.

Another famous family of Danville were the Vandegrifts, who moved there in 1861. Frances "Fanny" Vandegrift married the famous author and poet Robert Louis Stevenson. Fanny was born in a house on Indianapolis' Monument Circle in 1840. She recalled playing in the abandoned halls of the first governor's mansion built on the Circle and recognized as Indianapolis' first haunted house.

In Plainfield, on the grounds of the Friends' Meetinghouse, 205 S. East St., set back in a park bordering the south side of Main St. (US 40), there once stood an elm tree, known as the Van Buren Elm. In 1842, while making a political swing, ex-president Martin Van Buren arrived in Plainfield via the National Road (US 40). At this site, his stagecoach struck the roots of the old elm tree and overturned, spilling the former president into the mud.

Danville's Creature From Hell

Although the Avon Bridge on US 37 near Danville is well known in recent folklore as a haunted site (see "you'll also want to see"), Danville residents claim their railroad bridge further down the road from the Avon Bridge over Whitelick Creek is the "real" haunted bridge in the county. Could it be that during the building of *both* bridges that each had an accident-prone workman who fell and was entombed alive in freshly poured cement supports? Stranger things have happened, and they have happened in Danville.

One story that circulated in Danville in 1883 was still being told in the 1930s. When the story was first told, Danville was a small eighty-acre community only a little over fifty years old. The surrounding area still had dense forests, and hunting was a frequent pastime.

Newspapers reported that a couple of friends from Danville decided to go rabbit hunting. As they entered the forest just west of the city they were in high spirits. The weather was perfect and they anticipated having a successful hunting day.

They neared the heart of the woods. At first they noticed how still it had become. There was absolutely no sound even in the underbrush, as if every wild creature was in hiding. They slowly proceeded. Then they heard something. Thinking it was game of some kind they began to stalk it, unaware that they, too, were being stalked.

Then they heard the sound of hoofs pounding toward them. No horseman in his right mind would bring a horse into this thicket, let alone at the speed this one was approaching.

Suddenly and horrifyingly bursting from the black heart of the forest they saw a creature which could only be said to have come from HELL! Turning they ran for their lives with the creature right behind them. Somehow they reached the edge of the forest and burst through, panting and nearly dead of fright.

When they returned to Danville and told their story, no one believed them at first, then others began reporting sightings of the demonic creature from hell appearing in the surrounding forests.

What was this creature? It was black as black could be, frightened victims said, a horselike creature with streams of pale blue light shooting from its eyes. Its mane and tail were made of black, writhing snakes and its forked tongue shot out fire! Some hunters reported seeing huge wings of zebra-striped feathers. The creature could climb trees from which it would drop down onto unwary intruders of its domain.

Today, Danville may claim to have a haunted bridge, but that is nothing compared to what it once had: a creature from Hell!

❋❋❋

You'll Also Want to See:

The Haunted Avon Bridge and White Lick Bridge, over White Lick Creek. From Indianapolis go west on Rockville Road (Rockville will become US 36) for several stoplights. After the intersection with SR 267 continue west on 36. After a few miles you will come to the intersection of 36 and East Main Street (Old 36). Turn left onto Twin Bridges Road. The bridge you will go under as the road twists and turns is the old Haunted Avon Bridge, and White Lick Bridge is beyond it.

Could one of these workers be the man, entombed alive in one of the bridge's supports, who still is said to haunt the Avon bridge?

Photos courtesy of the Avon-Washington Township Public Library

HENRY COUNTY

Henry County was named for Patrick Henry and settled primarily by early Quakers in 1821. The county seat, New Castle, was platted in 1836 and named by Ezekiel Leavell, an early settler, for his home, New Castle, Kentucky. The novel *Raintree County* by Hoosier Ross Lockridge Jr. is supposed to be set in Henry County.

New Castle grew along agricultural and small business lines. During the early part of the twentieth century the city was known as the "Rose City" because it was the major grower and distributor of the American Beauty Rose. At one time there were more than fifty greenhouses and twice as many florists located in the city.

The city's history changed dramatically with the arrival of the auto industry and the establishment of the Hoosier Kitchen Cabinet Company. In 1907 such classic cars as the Maxwell, comedian Jack Benny's favorite car, Lawter and Universal were produced in New Castle. Chrysler Corporation purchased the Maxwell plant and continues to be the areas largest employer. Perfect Circle automotive company was headquartered at New Castle.

A testament to Hoosiers' dedication to and love of basketball can be seen at the Indiana Basketball Hall of Fame Museum built in New Castle in 1989. New Castle boasts the "largest high school gymnasium in the world." Officially it can seat 9,325, though crowds often top 10,000. Among the school's star alumni are Kent Benson and Steve Alford.

Spiceland, settled by North Carolina Quakers in 1820, was platted in 1850 and named for the abundance of spicebushes that grew in the area, often to a height of fifteen feet. The spicebush once covered central Indiana. Early settlers used the bark and fruit as a substitute for store tea.

The Knightstown Academy, a three-story red brick building constructed in the centennial year of 1876, served as one of the finest private schools in the state. Unique models of a telescope and one of a globe, symbolizing education and science, top the twin towers of the Second Empire-style structure.

The Haunted City

New Castle, Indiana, has had a modern-sounding missing child mystery haunting the town for eighty-nine years. The story began March 20, 1913, and resulted in a nation-wide search, coast-to-coast newspaper coverage and the writing of two songs.

A measles epidemic had closed the schools, and the students made plans for their unexpected vacation. However, for one family and the community of New Castle, this day would end with the disappearance of a nine-year-old girl and begin the haunting mystery which persists to this day.

Catherine Winters, the daughter of a local dentist, left her home on North 16th Street and walked six blocks to the Courthouse Square, where she joined friends and played in a friend's backyard. Shortly after 11:00 AM she began walking home for lunch. A family friend who saw her and waved was the last person to see Catherine Winters—or at least to admit seeing her that fateful day. At noon on a bright and sunny day, Catherine Winters vanished from the busiest street in town.

By that evening, the entire community knew of her disappearance. A preliminary search of the downtown areas failed to turn up any clues or anyone else who had seen her after the family friend's sighting. The police questioned everyone at local hotels, railroad stations and campgrounds about any strangers who might have left town that afternoon. A band of gypsies had been seen passing through town headed east toward Hagerstown about the time of her disappearance.

It was a time in Indiana when gypsies still roved freely through villages, staging entertainment, telling fortunes and causing distrust and contempt. It was rumored they stole children for the purpose of teaching them to steal for them.

The police, Dr. Winters and some of his friends set out toward Hagerstown in hope of overtaking the gypsy wagons. Just after dark they found their camp. After questioning every member of the band and thoroughly searching their wagons, they left with no clues.

The day after her disappearance all New Castle businesses closed. More than six hundred people conducted a house-to-house search. Gypsy wagons throughout the Midwest were stopped and searched. Her stepmother consulted clairvoyants. Her father spent much of his life savings in an attempt to find his daughter.

The disappearance became front-page news for many large city papers, including the *Chicago Tribune* and the *Seattle Star*. Seventy other papers across the nation offered a $1,000 reward for information. Handbills were passed out in movie theaters throughout the country.

A year after Catherine's disappearance, the New Castle police chief obtained a warrant to search the Winters' home. A red sweater and hair bow were found concealed in the cellar wall.

A man who'd been boarding with the Winters at the time of Catherine's disappearance was arrested, along with her parents. The police were convinced her body was buried in the basement, but gave up after a search that netted no remains. Due to insufficient evidence, charges were dropped against the boarder and Catherine's parents.

Dr. Winters resumed his dental practice. Both he and his wife remained in the house until their deaths; the doctor died in 1940 and his wife in 1953.

In October 2000 bones were discovered between a wall in a downtown New Castle building. Rumors and speculations ran through the community. Had Catherine finally been found? The bones, however, turned out to be not human.

New Castle still is haunted by the mysterious disappearance of Catherine Winters.

❋❋❋

Two songs were written about the disappearance of Catherine Winters. The first of these—"Where Did Catherine Winters Go?"—was written by the Gorbett brothers in 1914. On the cover of the sheet music was a picture of the little girl surrounded by a heart shaped wreath of flowers and the words "dedicated to Catherine Winters, nine years of age, who disappeared from the streets of New Castle, Indiana, March 20, 1913 at eleven o'clock AM."

Where Did Catherine Winters Go?
(Words by Z. F. Gorbett and Music by Sylvester Gorbett)

There's a mystery in New Castle,
tell us truly if you know,
why did Catherine Winters leave us
and the friends that loved her so?
Merry birds sing 'round her homestead,
flowers bloom, friends come and go;
but the mystery in New Castle is
Where did Catherine Winters go?

Telephones were busy ringing,
quickly news flashed through the town
that the Winters girl was missing,
and no where could she be found.
Willing hearts, some teardrops falling,
spread the news for miles around:
Have you seen the little darling,
who is missing from our town?

Would you know her if you see her,
as through foreign lands you roam?
Here's her picture on this title;
if you do, please send her home.
Holy angels tell us truly.
Has she now a home with God?
Is her spirit with the angels,
and her form beneath the sod?

[Chorus]
Is she far away in bondage,
controlled by cruel hands?
Or is she among the angels,
in that holy land?
As for her, our hearts do yearn.
Roses bloom in all their beauty;
but will Catherine e'er return?

JOHNSON COUNTY

Johnson County, created in 1822 and named for early Indiana State Supreme Court Judge John Johnson, is currently home to over 100,000 Hoosiers. Johnson County townships include Blue River, Clark, Franklin, Hensley, Needham, Nineveh, Pleasant, Union and White River. Franklin is the county seat. Other cities and towns include Bargersville, Edinburg, Franklin, Greenwood, New Whiteland, Princess Lake, Trafalger and Whiteland.

The first white settler, John Campbell, arrived in 1820 and built a cabin in Edinburg. A plaque marks the site on Kyle Street. Johnson County is the home of what became the largest cannery west of Baltimore. In 1872 Johnson County residents James T. and Laura B. Polk started the "Polk's Best" brand of canned vegetables by canning tomatoes on their kitchen stove. "Polk's Best" were sold world wide for many years.

Johnson County enjoys the distinction of being one of the few that had a company enlisted in the 1832 Black Hawk War. The campaign was short, and was devoid of any bloody experiences. The company consisted of about 100 men, and marched from here to Chicago, near which place they remained in camp several weeks. They were ordered back home at the end of two months, having sustained no loss except a few horses which were stolen by the Indians.

Johnson County also had a company enlisted in the Mexican War (1846-1848). The company lost about fifteen men, nearly all to disease.

Little Girl in the Window

In April 1997, a nineteenth-century, twenty-four-room Gothic revival home was on the move after being rescued by the Historic Landmarks Foundation of Indiana. The gingerbread-decorated cottage was being moved from Mills and Mann Roads to Southport and Mann Roads.

When an *Indianapolis Star* photographer's camera caught the image of a little blond girl in a blue dress looking out of an upstairs window, many callers to the *Star* were certain he had photographed a ghost.

The reporter stated he thought he'd seen a little girl in the window, but knew that was impossible. He decided that it was a play of light or curtains reflecting—but not a ghost!

If it were the picture of a little girl's ghost what would she have been thinking?

Shortly after the picture appeared in the paper, rumors began circulating that a little girl had died in an accident in the house or some other tragedy had befallen her. Research proved, however, that no little girl had ever died in this house.

The ghostly figure of a little girl watches as "her" house is moved from Mills and Mann Roads to Southport and Mann Roads.

Photo by *Indianapolis Star* photographer, Mike Fender.

MADISON COUNTY

Madison County was chartered in 1823, two years after the last of the Delaware Indians, who had populated the vicinity for about three quarters of a century, left, treaty-bound for new homes in Kansas. A series of shifts in the county's border brought it to its present rectangular shape by 1838. Today Madison is Indiana's sixth most populated county.

Madison County lay at the core of the largest natural gas field in the United States, covering more than 5,000 square miles. John D. Stephenson and William Conner laid out Alexandria in 1836. The town was probably named for the ancient city of Alexandria, or perhaps for the wife of one of the founders. In 1887 the county's first gas well was drilled near Alexandria.

Anderson, platted in 1823, was first named Andersontown, for William Anderson, a Delaware chief, whose Indian name was *Kikthawenund*, "Making a Cracking Noise." The Delaware name for the area was *Wapiminskink*, "Chestnut Tree Place." Early settlers referred to Anderson either by his Christian name, William, or as Captain Anderson. He was a prominent Indian leader and negotiated several major Delaware treaties with the United States. In 1818 he reluctantly signed the St. Mary's Treaty, relinquishing Delaware land claims in Indiana. Within three years after this agreement most Delaware had left Andersontown.

William Conner, a son-in-law of Chief Anderson, sold 320 acres, which included the abandoned Delaware village, to John Berry. Berry surveyed and platted Andersontown in 1823 and in 1828 the county government was located there. In 1848 the name was changed to Anderson. Anderson today is a fast-growing suburban community of Indianapolis.

Wendell Willkie (1892–1944), the unsuccessful Republican Party candidate for the presidency in 1940, was born in Elwood in Madison County. During the 1940 campaign the Republican candidate won only nine states in the Electoral College; however, he won 45 percent of the popular vote, more than two predecessors who had opposed Franklin Roosevelt. Willkie wrote a book, *One World* (1943), which called for a unified world order. He died unexpectedly in 1944 and was buried at Rushville, where his home may be visited at the corner of A and 19th Streets.

Nineteenth Century Eccentric Ghost Tales

Madison County seemed a particularly superstitious place during the nineteenth century, with spooky legends abounding. According to one of these legends Delaware Chief Anderson's ghost kept a watchful eye over the community that bears his name. The chief's intervention is reputed to be responsible for the city's never having been seriously damaged by tornadoes.

Storytellers say that more than a hundred years ago, when the clouds gathered and the sky grew dark, the ghost of Chief Anderson appeared on the roof of the Meridian Hotel, across from the police station. He slowly raised his arms toward the sky and the storm clouds lifted above the city and moved on.

Today no one knows where the chief performs this feat if bad weather advances, since the Meridian Hotel, 709-711 Meridian Street, is now a parking lot.

In May 1894 the *Elwood Daily Press* printed a story concerning the sightings of ghosts in the vicinity of Elwood. Several farmers returning from the city after dark were passing an old gas well set back from the road when they saw the ghost of a man, a giant. As they watched, a young woman appeared—another apparition—in a white flowing gown, and with long dark hair. The woman and the giant appeared to talk to each other and then the giant grabbed her and thrust a knife into her heart. Blood flowed down her white gown, and then, the apparitions disappeared.

Spiritualists believed they knew who the giant specter was and why he committed the ghostly murder. Much earlier an oil worker had died in an accident while working on the gas well. The giant specter was an ancestor of his and was avenging the wrongs done to the workman by a woman.

Not too long after the Elwood story appeared, the *Anderson Democrat* printed a similar story. Two farmers on their way home encountered the giant at the edge of a small woods about two miles east of Markleville. They, too, bore witness to a grisly ghostly murder enacted before their eyes. When they finally arrived at their homes, they told others what they'd seen but were scoffed at.

However, it did arouse interest. The following evening three or four of the neighbors went to the spot. After watching for several hours, they were just about ready to give up and go home when in the center of the road appeared the form of a giant man no less than ten feet tall!

A few seconds after the giant appeared a second figure slowly materialized—a beautiful woman with black hair flowing down her back, wearing a long billowing white gown. They stood looking at each other when suddenly the giant grabbed her and plunged a knife into her heart. The woman fell to the ground, blood covering her gown. The giant dropped the knife beside her and then disappeared.

The group of men rushed to where the woman had fallen and as they approached she vanished. There was no sign of the knife or the blood. Could they have been dreaming a "dream most foul?"

This time spiritualists who were consulted could give no explanation for the nomadic specters.

On January 26, 1896, the *Anderson Herald* published an account of another Madison County ghost sighting near the town of Florida.

The ghost appeared nightly, roaming through a forty-acre field that belonged to the widow of Isaac Osborne. During his lifetime Mr. Osborne had an ongoing feud with his neighbor, Isaiah Bodkins. Before his death he gave his wife instructions "not to sell Bodkins that forty acres nor let him lease it." If she did, he would come back in spirit form and walk the land until Bodkin relinquished his claim.

A few years after Osborne's death his widow did agree to rent the forty acres to Bodkins, going against her husband's dying wishes. Shortly after Bodkins began working the land, a ghostly form began prowling over the land from night until morning. Also, Bodkins and two of his friends saw a peculiar light flitting about the field.

People in the neighborhood would drive far out of their way after dark in order to avoid the haunted farm. When Bodkins decided to relinquish the land, the apparition and strange light disappeared and was never seen again.

Stories of the ghostly giant and his beautiful victim continued circulating into the 1920s with a few slight variations and then disappeared.

❋❋❋

Sam Maag . . . Is it You?

Sam Maag built his two-story white frame farmhouse in 1898 on land, according to county histories, once occupied by a small Indian village. He, his wife and a boy named Chester, whom they were raising, lived there and farmed the land for many years. Sadly, Chester died young. He was laid out in the parlor as was customary during that time.

For many years the Maags continued to live in the house until Sam's death. Finally his widow made the decision to sell. The house was just what the Morrills were looking for. Purchasing it in 1958, they and their two daughters, Toni and Nikki, moved in.

Neither Toni nor her sister remembers when or why they became convinced that the house was haunted. However, Nikki remembers that not too long after they'd moved in, she was awakened during the night to the vision of a man standing in the doorway of her bedroom. Thinking it was her father, she called out to him but got no response. The figure began to walk toward her bed. Frightened, Nikki ducked under the covers. When she peeked out again the figure was gone.

There were no other sightings until one day in 1990, when Toni saw an image in the basement that "turned and faded into the door."

Toni admits that as a child she was afraid of the house. There were noises. The most frequent and common of these over the years was footsteps on the stairs. Both girls had told their parents they believed that the house was haunted. They began calling the ghost Sam. Their father attributed the "disturbances" to overactive youthful imaginations.

One evening the father was home alone when *he* heard the footsteps on the stairs. This disturbance was confirmed by the rapt attention of the dog, watching the stairs. Just as the last footstep was heard, the canine rose, walked toward the steps and wagged his tail. The girls' father became a believer.

As teenagers the sisters conducted their own séance in an attempt to discover the ghost's identity. Lighting six candles and turning out the lights, they began asking the ghost if he were Sam Maag or the boy, Chester. Nothing happened during the experiment. As they turned the lights on all six candles blew out AND the lights went out. The girls left the room in a hurry.

When Toni married, her parents converted the upstairs into an apartment for the young couple. Her husband laughed at her stories that the house was haunted until one morning he awoke to find their triple dresser moved several feet from the wall and sitting beside the bed.

When Toni's daughter was about two, the little girl went into the kitchen one morning where Toni was fixing breakfast and asked, "Who is that man?" Toni, perplexed by the question, asked the little girl to take her to where the man was. The little girl took her into the other room and pointed into a corner where Toni saw . . . no one. She decided it was Sam.

Toni, now divorced, still lives in Sam Maag's house and can recount continuing instances of strange happenings. One of Sam's "jokes" is to open the china cabinet door. Once this happened when an insurance salesman was sitting at the table. He was curious as to what happened. How could the door open all by itself? "It's just our ghost" was the explanation he received. He quickly completed his business and left.

"Good Night, Mr. 'G'"

Only tour guide Barb Lumbis is willing to stay alone in Madison County's Gruenewald Historic House, located at 626 Main Street in Anderson. As a matter of fact, the house's board of commissioners passed a ruling that two people must be present in the house when it is open. This mandate was the result of an unsettling incident experienced by a volunteer.

In an October 30, 1994 article, published in the *Herald Bulletin*, Mrs. Lumbis told about one of her ghostly encounters in the house. There was no one else in the house but the volunteer, who felt that she was being followed about. At one point she was certain that the presence had positioned itself between her and the door, though she saw nothing. Afraid to move, she was finally able to get to the door. She flung the door open and ran from the house and refused to return.

The board brought in a medium, who "felt" two spirits in the house.

One of them, the medium said, was the last owner, Martin Gruenewald. The other she thought would not stay long and was probably the Gruenewald's granddaughter, Wilhelmina. When Wilhelmina was alive, she never agreed with any proposed plans for changing the historic home. It was probably she who stood between the volunteer and the door.

Barb Lumbis said that it's not unusual for a volunteer to enter the house and find the electric typewriter typing by itself. Once while in the kitchen having lunch with her parents, Barb heard someone come into the house and go up the stairs. When she went up to see who it was, there wasn't anyone around.

The image of Mr. Gruenewald that Barb Lumbis said she once saw was wearing formal attire. The apparition appears mostly on the second floor, or sometimes it is reflected in a mirror.

Each night when Barb leaves she always calls out, "Good night Mr. 'G.'"

❋❋❋

Miss Robert's Mansion

The Inness mansion located on Alexandria's south side at 601 S. Indiana Avenue was built by John Inness, who died shortly after the house was completed, leaving a pregnant wife, Mary and daughter, Blanche.

John had already named the unborn child Robert—they had "known" it was going to be a boy. Although the baby turned out to be a little girl, Mary decided to honor her husband's request and named her Robert Inness.

When the girls grew up, older daughter Blanche became an opera singer; she traveled the world with her husband. Her sister Robert continued to live in the Inness home.

As time moved on, both the mother and Blanche died. Miss Robert continued living in the home as a recluse until sometime in the 1960s, when she was no longer able financially—or physically—to maintain the property. Bob Wilhite purchased the home with the stipulation that Miss Robert could stay until her death, which came in 1977. Wilhite spent many hours cleaning the yard and renovating the home. But before he'd completed the task, he died in 1983.

Charles Sanqunetti had always been fascinated by the Inness house. He'd peer into the overgrown bushes toward the house and imagine it was haunted. After Wilhite's death Charles and his wife, Barb, decided to buy the mansion.

Charles admits that most incidents that make the house seem to be haunted can be explained away as squirrels scurrying about. There are, however, a few incidents that defy explanation. He feels distinct taps on his shoulder, and when he turns around no one is there. Then, there are the heavy footsteps heard upstairs in unoccupied rooms.

Probably the one occurrence that made Barb a believer happened when Charles was in the kitchen on a ladder and felt a distinct cold draft blow across the ceiling. He got down from the ladder to close the door but found all the doors closed. Then he found his wife standing at the bottom of the stairs leading to the second floor, unwilling to go any further. She felt or sensed something or someone was preventing her from moving.

Barb admits that there's one room upstairs that makes her feel particularly uncomfortable. It's a pretty bedroom decorated with Victorian furnishings, and an antique dress placed across the bed. The dress found in the attic, is believed to have been Blanche's.

One day Charles and his wife entered their second floor bedroom and were startled by a bat flying around their new entertainment center and then disappearing. Suddenly, the entertainment center began rocking back and forth and the doors on the cabinet flew open. The rocking continued for several seconds. No earthquake had been reported anyplace in the county that day.

One night they had fallen asleep on a couch in front of the fireplace in the living room. Early in the morning they were both awakened by the sound of footsteps walking across the room above them. Charles likened the sound to that made by the old boot-style shoes schoolteachers used to wear. Even their dogs stared up at the ceiling, listening.

The top of the stairs and particularly the bathroom were also "sensitive" areas. Once, a medium visited and told Barb there was definitely a presence in that area as well as in the bedroom. She also confirmed Charles' belief that the kitchen—where he had felt a draft and where Barb admitted to having seen a "wispy thing"—was another sensitive area. Though the medium couldn't tell them if there is more than one presence or who it is, Charles and Barb are certain that no harm is intended.

Cold drafts, the sound of a footsteps and a "wispy thing" floating from room-to-room convinced the Sanqunettis that Miss Robert is with them.

Photo by Charles Sanqunetti

You'll also want to see:

Mounds State Park on Mounds Road in Anderson. Deep in the park is a celestial observatory decorated with odd symbols, some of which are unknown, but one has been identified as the fiery comet snake. And if you know where to look you will find a circle where sun-worshipping rites were probably conducted. You can also see there ten distinct earthworks from around 200 B.C. built by Adena-Hopewell people.

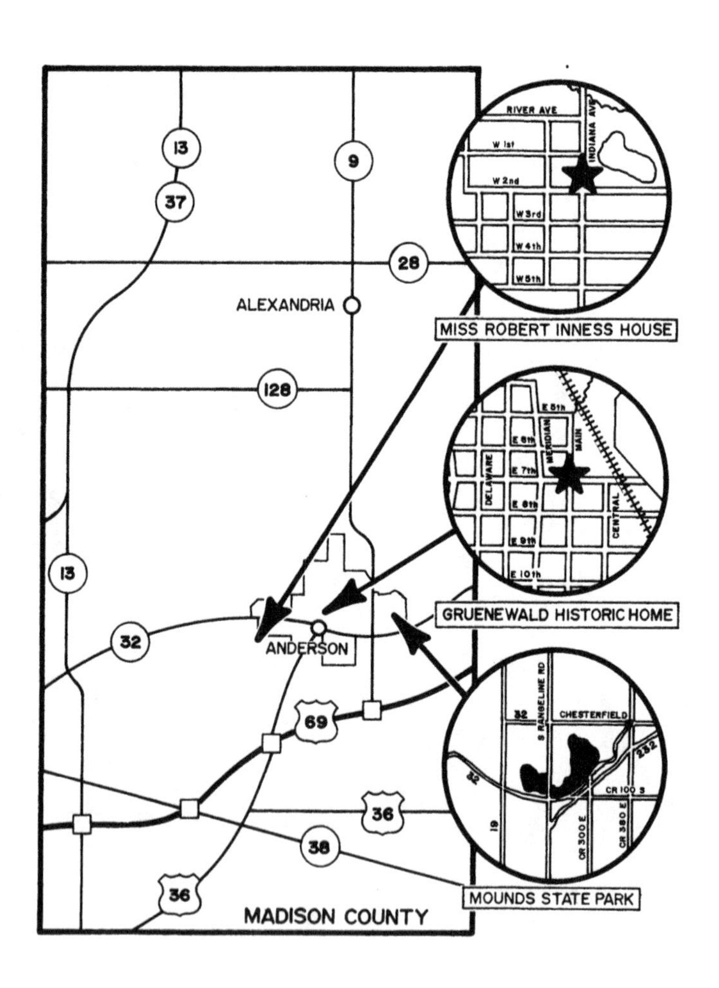

MARION COUNTY

Marion County was organized in 1822 and named for General Francis "Swamp Fox" Marion, an officer in the American Revolution.

In the 1820s Alexander Ralston and Elias P. Fordham surveyed a site in central Indiana suggested by the Conner Commission. Ralston, who assisted in laying out Washington, D.C., is probably most responsible for the exemplary plan of Indianapolis. In the middle of the new capital they placed a circle, which was to be the center of the town's activities. The Indiana Soldiers and Sailors Monument, dedicated in 1902, occupies the site.

By the 1830s Indianapolis was a major stopping point for traffic moving west on the National Road. Hopes for the Central Canal that would link the capital to the Wabash and Erie Canal were dropped due to the depression of 1837. The only portion of the canal to be finished extended from the village of Broad Ripple to Indianapolis. Railroads succeeded where the canal had failed. The first train from Madison arrived in Indianapolis in 1847 and Indianapolis became a national center of railroad traffic.

Indianapolis' name also became linked with the automobile industry. More than seventy different automobiles were manufactured in the city including the Cole, Duesenberg, Stutz and Marmon. Today that tradition is continued at the Indy 500, the Brickyard 400 and the Formula One. Today Indiana's capital city is a center of education, sports activities, manufacturing and new biotech initiative industries.

The Acton Miracle

"I don't know what it was that happened that night," Bob says, "but it surely was a miracle."

Bob recently had lost his father and other family problems were weighing heavily on his mind and heart as he rode his motorcycle on I-74 near Acton. Storm clouds darkened the sky and it began to rain. He stopped along the shoulder of the highway to put on his rain gear.

Shocked motorists watched as a bolt of blue-white lightning hurled toward the earth and struck the man struggling into his rain gear. One of them called the police and reported the lightning strike. Paramedics from Acton quickly responded to the call. When they arrived they found Bob lying along the roadside; his body gray and apparently lifeless. His shoes had been blown off, and steam was coming from his wounds.

The paramedics checked for vitals and found the man had no pulse. His life seemed to have slipped away. One of the paramedics began CPR while another one called for the Lifeline helicopter. Meanwhile, the torrential storm continued, the heavy dark clouds obscuring the daylight, thunder and threatening lightning crackling in the atmosphere.

The motorcyclist was not responding to the CPR efforts of the paramedic when they received word that the Lifeline helicopter couldn't come due to the severe storm.

A crowd of bystanders silently watched the paramedics continuing their efforts to get a response from the motorcyclist. Suddenly a woman in a long black dress, resembling the style of another era, a Bible clutched tightly to her heart, pushed her way through the group of bystanders.

"I must touch him!" She murmured. Thinking the woman must be a relative, a paramedic called out, "Let her through. Let her do what she has to do."

The woman knelt beside the motionless body, pounding her Bible on Bob's chest, speaking words that no one could quite hear in the midst of the loud thunder and lightning and torrential downpour.

For no apparent reason the ambulance lights dimmed and the emergency equipment failed. The woman looked up, smiled, rose and disappeared into the crowd of onlookers. The paramedic monitoring the motorcyclist's vitals detected a pulse. Suddenly the rain stopped, the sky cleared and the ambulance lights came back on.

"It was a miracle, there's no other word for it," stated one of the paramedics.

The helicopter arrived and transported the injured man to the hospital, where he spent seven weeks in a coma. Once awakened from his coma, the motorcyclist faced several weeks of therapy. Today he's healthy. But who, he still wonders, was the mysterious lady in black?

Was the woman an angel sent from God, a ghost, a spirit or a vision? Some citizens in the Acton community feel that there may be a connection between the old Acton Campground and the woman in black.

Relics of the campground, once located at the corner of Acton and Southport Roads, are preserved in the Franklin Township Historical Museum. Also there is a black dress that fits the description of the dress worn that night.

An Acton resident donated the black dress, a late 1800s style, to the museum in the late 1970s. The donor had purchased the home of a doctor, which still contained some of the original owner's furniture, and the dress was found hanging in an upstairs closet. After both the doctor and his wife's death, a niece inherited the house and lived there until she was found murdered, a crime that was never solved. What, if anything, does this black dress have to do with the events on I-74?

The forty-acre Acton Campground, which opened in the late 1850s, was located near the present intersection of Acton Road and Southport Road (northwest corner). The Acton Campground was intended to be used primarily for evangelical revival meetings of the Methodist Episcopal Church. During its existence people traveled from Indianapolis, Shelbyville and Greensburg to attend the meetings, coming by roads and the Big Four Railroad, which bordered the grounds.

Hundreds of people came to the campgrounds to hear speakers like evangelist T. DeWitt Talmage and Sam Jones and to listen to the music. Staying in the hotel or in tents or the cabins, they became a close-knit, devout community until a tragic fire in 1905 destroyed all of the buildings.

Could the woman in the black dress have been one of those devout Christians still waiting for the Acton Campground to be rebuilt?

Who was the mysterious woman in black who performed the miracle on I-74? Could this dress, which was donated to the Franklin Township Historical Museum, be hers?

Photo courtesy of Sylvia C. Henricks, Vice President, Franklin Township Historical Museum.

❋❋❋

The Alverna Retreat Ghost

The Alverna Retreat House operated by the Franciscans had been located on Springmill Road on the north side of Indianapolis for many years.

Although it might seem odd that a ghost would choose to haunt a Franciscan retreat, stories still circulate that the shy ghost of one of Indianapolis' most prominent men haunted the building.

A housekeeper saw the ghost. She had been cleaning sinks in the basement bathroom when the door opened. Out of the corner of her eye she thought she saw someone enter the room and she told him to wait a moment and she'd be through. Turning to look at him, she saw no one—he just wasn't there anymore.

The housekeeper had only a brief glance, but recalled that he had white hair and wore a black jacket, dark pants, a white shirt with no buttons and a black cap.

The housekeeper wasn't the only one who had seen this ghost. A former secretary at the retreat saw a similarly clad figure standing in the solarium. When she asked one of the fathers who he was, she was told there wasn't anyone at that time in the retreat who matched her description.

One day one of the fathers was going through Oldfields, the Lilly Pavilion of the Decorative Arts located at the Indianapolis Museum of Art, when he saw a portrait of Hugh McKenna Landon. In the portrait, Landon wore a sailing outfit that consisted of a black jacket, dark pants, a white turtleneck sweater and a sailing cap. This matched the housekeeper's description of the man that the secretary and housekeeper had "seen."

Landon had been the original owner of Oldfields before he sold the home to J. K. Lilly, who later gave it to the art museum. After selling Oldfields, Landon built a turreted mansion on forty-six acres of land, which after his death was purchased by the Franciscans and converted to the Alverna Retreat.

Though the fathers never admitted that the ghost existed and could not explain the sightings, they did acknowledge that the description given by both ladies did match that of the man in Landon's portrait.

Neither of the two women had ever met Landon and did not know the house's history. However, they both believed that the man they saw was indeed Mr. Landon. While they both worked for the Franciscans he would appear before them from time to time and on at least one occasion even smiled at the housekeeper.

They both agreed that they didn't feel fearful. They sensed a kind of shyness to him and a sense of friendliness. They believed he just wanted them to know that he was still there and was enjoying his retreat. Today the Alverna Retreat is a private housing development.

※※※

The Girl in White

It was late, dark and pouring rain. Not a fit night even for ducks. There wasn't another car in sight. Probably everyone else was at home cozy, watching TV. The man was tired and couldn't wait to put the car in the garage, warm up a TV dinner and relax with the news.

The stoplight at the corner of Michigan Road and 38th Street had turned yellow. The man began slowing down the car until it came to a stop at the intersection just as the light changed to red.

Out of the corner of his eye he saw something white. Turning his head toward Crown Hill Cemetery, he saw her standing there in the deluge as if she were waiting for a ride. She was dressed in what appeared to be a long white satin prom dress, and just peeking out from under the hemline were the toes of dainty satin slippers.

He rolled down his window and called to her asking if she needed a ride. She nodded and walked to the car, opened the door and got into the back seat. As they pulled away from the corner she gave him directions to her home and then was silent. No matter how much he tried to engage her in conversation she just sat there looking out the window. The car was as silent as if he were alone.

When he pulled up in front of the house to which she had directed him, he looked into the rearview mirror: horrors! she had vanished!

Unnerved (quite naturally), the man went up to the house and knocked on the door. An elderly couple opened the door and he explained what had happened, describing the girl. The elderly couple turned pale and began to cry. The woman walked away from the door and when she returned she showed him a framed photograph of a smiling beautiful young girl in a white prom dress. He was shocked! This was the girl he'd picked up at the corner of Crown Hill Cemetery.

The couple explained that the photo was of their daughter who had died in an auto accident several years earlier. It had been a rainy night when she and her boyfriend left the house on their way to the senior prom. She was buried in Crown Hill Cemetery.

This wasn't the first time that strangers had knocked on their door. It had happened before. No one knows exactly when the story of the girl in white began. But, as the years passed, others reported seeing the girl in white standing in the rain just outside of Crown Hill Cemetery at the corner of Michigan Road and 38th Street. Since this story seems to be told in other cities, it qualifies as an urban ghost story.

※※※

The Haunting of Beck House

On March 11, 1962, what had been a typical quiet Sunday in Indianapolis began to literally shatter at approximately 10:37 PM. The Beck family—a grandmother, mother and teenage daughter—were all in the kitchen when they heard a resounding crash upstairs.

Mystified, they climbed the stairs to the grandmother's room. There they found a heavy crystal vase, which the grandmother had brought with her from her home in Germany, was lying on the floor about four feet from a bookcase where it had been kept on the top shelf. The vase was broken to pieces! How did it manage on its own to get off the top shelf and land four feet away?

About forty-five minutes after they heard the vase crash to the floor, a heavy ashtray was flung violently against the wall in the living room!

After picking up the broken glass in both of the rooms, the three women returned to the kitchen. All too soon they again heard the sound of glass shattering upstairs. The Becks quickly gathered some clothing and went to a hotel.

The next morning, the Becks returned to their home and began cleaning up the broken glass. By 2:00 PM the breaking of glass resumed, both upstairs and downstairs, keeping the women on the run up and down the stairs, going from room to room to find bowls and vases broken. Finally, they called the police.

Sergeant John Mullin was the first to respond. When he arrived at the house at 2910 N. Delaware, he reported finding three very nervous, nearly hysterical women and a house littered with broken glass and china. He ventured the opinion that perhaps the damage had somehow been done either by a hi-fi or a pellet gun! This, of course, could not be the case. The house had no record player and since all of the windows were intact, the pellet gun theory was ridiculous.

That night Patrolman Ray Patton was dispatched to the house. As he stood in the house, the silence was broken by the sound of something falling in the daughter's bedroom. He found a glass figurine broken to pieces, lying in the center of the room.

He called for backup and high-frequency sound equipment. By the time the patrolmen and equipment arrived, they found hundreds of curious onlookers blocking the flow of traffic. Other police were dispatched to keep the street open.

The listening gear detected nothing out of the ordinary. During the time the equipment and officers were probing the house for answers, nothing happened. The investigative team departed, leaving Patrolman Patton with the family.

No sooner had the house and area around it been cleared, than the Becks and Patton heard a great crashing sound coming from upstairs. Patton raced up the steps with his gun drawn. There in one of the bedrooms lay the remains of a smashed mirror, heaped on the floor where it had fallen after evidently being knocked from the a wall by a glass that had been kept on the nightstand.

As the officer left the room and entered the hall, he was struck in the back of the head by a glass. Patton ran back into the bedroom and found another of the glasses broken on the floor. Lifting the hat where the three glasses had been hidden, he found only one left.

The strange activity continued for sixteen days. During that time police lieutenant Francis J. Dux was dispatched to the house. He firmly believed that the activity was a hoax, that one of the family members was responsible. Dux sat all the members of the household and their friends the Nosedas around the kitchen table and waited nearly ninety minutes without any new occurrences. Thus, convinced he had solved the "mystery," he was about to leave the kitchen when a beer stein sitting on the kitchen cabinet rose and dropped to the floor, breaking to pieces.

Then silverware began flying about the kitchen. Lieutennant Dux, the Becks and their friends moved to the living room for safety. After some time the sound of metal hitting the kitchen floor and walls ended, and they all reentered the kitchen only to find a chilling sight. There on the floor were three steak knives lying in the form of a cross. They had been kept in a drawer three feet from where they were found!

As they looked at the knives, they heard the furniture in the living room being moved about in a violent manner. But of course, none of the group was in that room.

As a last resort a priest was called in to perform an exorcism to rid the house of whatever had possessed it. After the exorcism the house was littered with fragments of mirrors, feathers from torn pillows, broken pottery and dented walls and woodwork where violently thrown objects had struck.

After the Beck family moved out, the house sat vacant for many years until it was purchased by another family twenty years later. The events, which had literally shattered a quiet Sunday evening, were never repeated. Evidently whatever was in the house when the Becks lived there had also moved. Today the house is gone. Nothing remains except a vacant lot.

The Murat Shrine Temple's Blue Light Special

The newly renovated Murat Shrine Temple has a ghost that is often described as a "shimmering blue light." Many performers have seen the light rising near the front of the theater at Delaware and Massachusetts, hovering and then dissipating. It is believed to be the ghost of Elias J. Jacoby, the Potentate at the time the mosque and theater were built in 1909. On December 31, 1935, Jacoby died as he was preparing to attend the temple's annual New Year's Eve party.

Stories of eerie blue lights hovering in the Murat Shrine Temple have been told for years. The light reportedly had been seen again and again, rising from one of the box seats and hovering near the stage. Some witnesses have reported seeing a "semi-transparent specter, seated in the front row of one of the balconies." Since the eerie blue light seemed to emanate from the area of Jacoby's favorite seat, the consensus seems to be that old Elias never left his beloved Murat Temple.

There is, however, much more to this spectral story. Workers have reported turning lights off and then finding them on again. Stage curtains have moved without anyone being near them. Elevators sometimes acted as if they had a mind of their own, and one night the chair in Jacoby's balcony was seen moving.

A young usher experienced a sighting of a different kind. Ignoring the rules, he'd gone backstage during a performance. As he peeked through a peephole in the curtain he saw an X-shaped black shadow just above one of the box seats. He was startled, but didn't think too much about it because stage lights are so bright that sometimes they blind someone on the stage for a moment.

Years later, after moving to New York City and landing a role with the road company of *Kismet*, the young usher found himself once again backstage at the Murat. He peeked out of the peephole and saw flashing from the ceiling of the theater and down to the floor that same "X"—obvious, it seemed, only to him.

Nearly forty years later, in 1989, he finally got some insight into the strange event, when he learned from a chance remark that a construction worker had fallen to his death when the theater was being constructed. The worker's outstretched arms and legs had formed an "X" when he landed in what was then the orchestra pit, just a few feet from the boxes where others have seen the eerie blue light.

The usher had a theory that the construction worker's death left behind an indelible print on the fabric of space or time, perceptible to those whose senses are somehow able to connect with this "image." Denying the possibility is akin to denying the existence of electricity because it can't be seen.

The most amazing story concerns Jacoby's portrait. In 1994 the Murat's public relations manager invited a group of psychics to spend the night in the temple. It was a perfect night for a ghost, with a full moon, but Jacoby's ghost didn't appear. That same night, however, the public relations manager froze in disbelief as he was gazing at Jacoby's portrait. Like a scene out of *The Picture of Dorian Gray*, he watched with amazement as the image on the painting first appeared to be a young man, then middle-aged, and then finally elderly.

He was beginning to question his sanity, or his eyesight, when a woman behind him said, "My God, he's crying," as she looked at the portrait. All in attendance that night swear that there had been a tear running down his cheek. Two months later, the announcement was made that the theater would be renovated.

But the story doesn't end here. During the renovation, a maintenance man high on a ladder looked down at the portrait and nearly fell. He swears Jacoby was looking up at him. Many employees and visitors to the facility insist that the eyes in Jacoby's portrait follow them.

Today, do those who operate and work at the Murat believe it's haunted? A guest services representative for the Murat described in a recent telephone conversation her introduction to the stories. It was seven years ago when she and other prospective employees were taken on a tour of the facilities. During this tour they were told that the upper floor was haunted and they were not to go up there. She never has.

Is Potentate Jacoby still at the Murat? Many say yes, at least in spirit.

The Slippery Noodle Inn

The Slippery Noodle Inn, built at 372 South Meridian Street in the 1850s, is listed on the National Register of Historic Places as Indianapolis' "oldest continuously operated bar in the original building at the original site." The Noodle, as it's fondly called, has received national recognition as one of the top twenty blues venues and is one of the "Best Blues Bars" in the nation.

The Noodle has hosted such celebrities as Hootie & the Blowfish, Billy Joel, Liza Minnelli, the John Mellencamp band (minus Mellencamp), and numerous sports figures. There have been a few visitors that have left hair-raising impressions on those who've encountered them. The historic building is reputed to be the site of many hauntings.

In the 1850s the Slippery Noodle Inn began its existence as the Tremont House, an inn and bar, providing accommodations for railroad passengers. Ten years later it was renamed Concordia House to honor the first German Lutheran immigrant ship to land in the New World—the *Concord*. It was later called the

Germania House and then Beck's Saloon. In 1963, the current owners, the Yeagy family, purchased the building.

Because the inn might have been a waystation on the Underground Railroad, or a bordello which was the site of a murder and was definitely the meeting place of both the Brady and Dillinger gangs (bullets can still be seen embedded in one of the brick walls), Hal Yeagy wonders if there are bodies buried in a basement area that he calls the "cubbyhole." No one seems to know the purpose of the cubbyhole. His employees try to avoid or hurry by this area, spooked by an aura emanating from the dark cavern.

In 1997 the Los Angeles coroner visited the Noodle and was taken on a tour of the building by Yeagy. After seeing the Dillinger/Brady "target" wall, the coroner was taken to the basement, where he stopped at the cubbyhole, and peering inside, backed up suddenly and said, "This place reeks of death."

The Noodle's kitchen manager arrives several hours before the other employees. One day, when he was in the basement, he looked up at the stairs and saw a six-foot-tall black man wearing coveralls looking down at him. As the manager approached him, the man disappeared! A week later the owner's son went into the basement. He soon came running up the stairs, pale and shaken. He, too, had encountered the tall man and watched him vanish!

Could this apparition be one of the many slaves who sought the next stop on the Underground Railroad? Perhaps the slave died before he could reach his destination. Or, could he be connected somehow with the gangster era of the building? We may never know who he is or why he's there. One thing is for certain—he seems to know he belongs at the Slippery Noodle Inn.

Indianapolis' First Haunted House

The first recorded haunted house in Indianapolis was the first governor's mansion, built on Monument Circle in 1829.

No governor, though, ever lived in this house. Governor James Ray was the first to be offered the opportunity; however, his wife flatly refused to live there, saying that every family in town would see her washing hanging on the line.

The mansion was used as offices for the Supreme Court judges. Judge Isaac Blackford rewrote the Indiana Code in his office there. For a time the State Library was housed in the building, as well as the State Bank.

It was soon left vacant, and the house began to deteriorate. Tramps slept in the deserted rooms and ladies of the night were said to also utilize these rooms.

By the late 1830s, when darkness fell on the city, people would shy away from the house, frightened by the stories of a ghost being seen and heard in the eerie shadows of the dusty rooms—thump—thump—thumping. Some said they'd seen it running past the windows and described it as a headless entity!

One cold November night a daring youth, Aaron Ohr, was taunted by his friends to go into the derelict house and capture the ghost—if he dared! Without hesitation or visible signs of fear he went inside while his friends bravely waited outside.

Soon they heard an awful racket: thumping and sounds like someone was being strangled—or worse! They were about ready to run away when out walked young Aaron. In his hand he held the ghost of the governor's mansion: the largest, the meanest looking wild turkey ever caught in Indianapolis.

Aaron took the turkey home. His mother cooked it and prepared the trimmings for a Hoosier Thanksgiving dinner and invited all of their friends to partake of the ghost of the governor's mansion.

❋❋❋

You'll Also Want to See:

The haunted Hannah House at 3801 Madison Avenue in Indianapolis, another stop on the Underground Railway where a disastrous fire is reputed to have loosed the spirits of some of the travelers hiding there. Also visit the old site of the famous House of Blue Lights.

For nearly forty years the home of prominent Indianapolis businessman Skiles Test was known as the House of Blue Lights. Though it no longer exists, the house at Fall Creek near Millersville Road was the most famous "haunted" house in Indianapolis in the 1950s and 1960s.

Stories circulated that Test's wife had died under mysterious circumstances and that he refused to allow her to be buried. Instead, she was dressed in a blue (her favorite color) ball gown, and placed in a glass coffin that sat upright in the living room. Blue lights creating an eerie blue glow illuminated the grounds, swimming pool and house. Another story concerned the small tombstones reported to be scattered throughout the property. Many Marion County teenagers had "ultimate adventure" experiences swarming over Mr. Test's property to see the sights and running around in the dark eluding local cops.

Trespassing curiosity seekers reported being shot at and chased by large vicious dogs. These stories became a "suburban" legend.

Test died March 18, 1964, and everything was sold at the largest auction ever held in the Midwest. Today the property is the Skiles Test Park. People claim they've seen a blue glow emanating from the heart of the park. Does the house still "exist?"

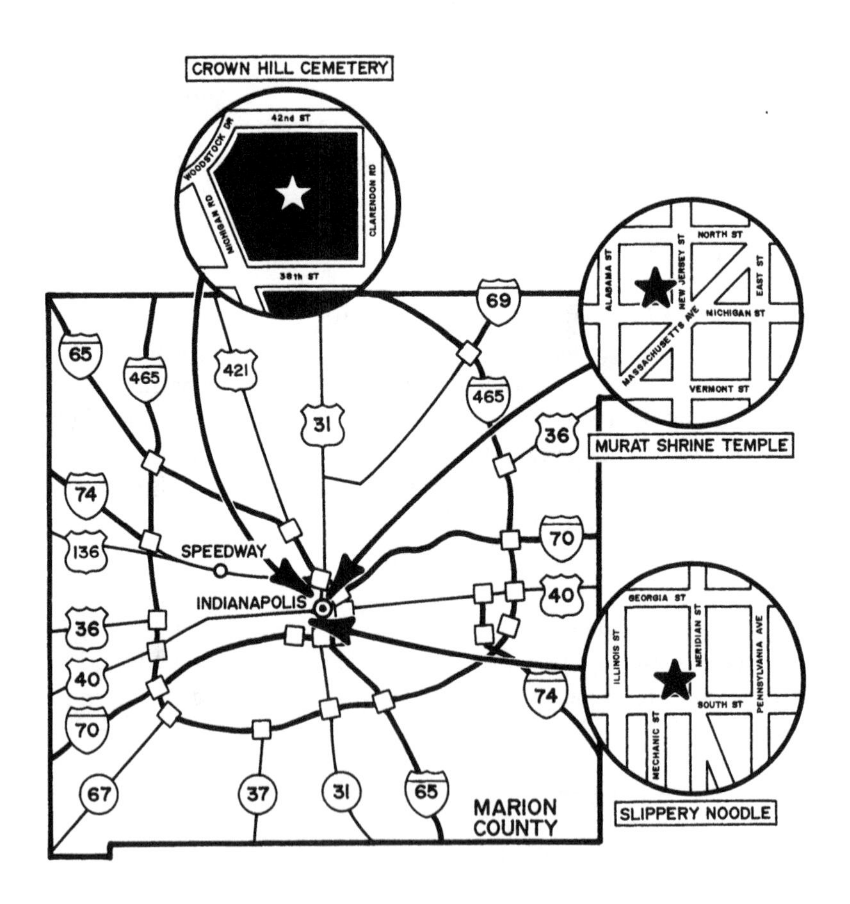

MONROE COUNTY

On January 14, 1818, the Indiana General Assembly formed Monroe County, named for President James Monroe, out of Orange County. In April that year the county commissioners established Bloomington, which had been settled in 1815, as the county seat.

Monroe County, located in the nation's most productive limestone belt, contains the state's largest inland body of water, Lake Monroe, and the vast Morgan-Monroe State Forest, which straddles the border between Morgan and Monroe Counties with the largest portion being in Monroe. This is the second largest forest in the state with 23,465 acres.

One of many historical sites in Bloomington is the Gables, a food establishment that has served as a student meeting point since 1919. Originally it was called the "Book Nook," and was made famous by local songwriter Hoagy Carmichael. It is believed that in this building is where he composed his famous song *Stardust*.

Stinesville was once a major center of Indiana limestone production, providing much of the stone used in the Soldiers and Sailors Monument in Indianapolis. The prosperity enjoyed by the community in the 1880s declined when a fire in 1916 destroyed the Hoadley stone mill.

Ellettsville was platted in 1837 and named for Edward Elletts, a local businessman. The community grew slowly until Englishman John Matthews established the first limestone industry in the area in 1862. Matthews, as an apprentice, had helped build London's Parliament houses.

The Haunted Morgan-Monroe State Forest

If buildings and cemeteries can be haunted why couldn't a state forest? The old Stepp Cemetery that rests within and belongs to the state forest reserve has received that reputation. Its pioneer spirits are believed to be restless.

Curious visitors can take the road through the forest, park and walk the path to the pioneer cemetery. Some visitors say they have seen a woman in black haunting the graveyard, sitting on a tree stump, watching over her young son's grave. Just in front of this stump is a small, sad tombstone bearing the inscription, Baby Lester.

The woman in black arrives after dusk and leaves before dawn. If a visitor arrives just at dusk or dawn he or she can sit in the stump seat and wait for the woman in black. But take warning, say the locals, for if one does, he or she may evoke "the curse"—and something terrible may happen.

Sometimes, they say, Baby Lester's glowing dog will appear to protect the child's grave.

MORGAN COUNTY

The Indiana legislature in 1821 created Morgan County from parts of what had been Delaware and Wabash Counties. The county was named for Brigadier General Daniel Morgan, a frontier hero of the American Revolution. Morgan County is well suited for farming; however, many in the county work in Indianapolis.

Martinsville, the county seat, was established in 1822 and named for one of the founders, John Martin, a member of the board of commissioners responsible for creating the county seat. Martinsville was once known nationally as the Artesian City for its mineral springs and health sanitariums.

With the decline of visitation at the several mineral water sanitariums in the area, Martinsville reverted to reliance on agriculture. In recent years the area has become the home of many Indianapolis commuters.

Two former Indiana governors grew up in Martinsville, Emmett Branch (1924–1925) and Paul V. McNutt, (1933–1937).

Mooresville, named for Samuel Moore and established as a utopian community in 1824, became the center of a farming community and is now an Indianapolis commuter suburb. Mooresville lays claim to having been the home of Paul Hadley, designer of the Indiana state flag. It is also noted for having in residence in 1920 the Dillinger family, who'd moved from Indianapolis to a farm near Mooresville. At that time their son, John Dillinger, later the notorious bank robber, was eighteen.

The Point of Death

Bridges seem to be a favorite spot for hauntings and encounters. It might be because a bridge represents a span over a difficult, dangerous, or unknown area beneath, symbolizing dangerous passages in life. Usually the haunting concerns an event that happened under the bridge, such as a drowning car accident. The traveler must go over the haunted bridge to meet the ghost or may expect the ghost on approaching, as in the case of the Mooresville Bridge.

Not unlike other haunted bridge stories in Indiana, this story tells of a worker falling into the fresh cement as the bridge was being built. Once entombed there was nothing to do but leave him there. In this case, there was a problem—one of the worker's arms was exposed, dangling from the support. His co-workers got a chain saw and simply cut off the arm and smeared some cement over the stump to blend it in with the rest of the structure. People in the area swear that from time to time the arm will appear, motioning. It may only point in some direction.

The location became a favorite parking spot for teens in the area. One night, so the story goes, there were a few cars parked there when suddenly the phantom arm appeared. The occupants in all of the cars saw the arm. They watched in horror as it rose in the air with its index finger extended. The arm moved from one car to the next and finally stopped at one of the cars, a blue Ford. It never moved again—just pointed at the blue Ford. All of the teens became frightened and drove away.

Three days later a car speeding down one of the graveled county roads lost control on a curve. The car rolled over and over into a cornfield, ending upside down. The farmer had been working out in his field at the time, but was unable to get to the two occupants before the car burst into flames. Both of the teens were killed.

The two were on their way to a high school football game when the accident occurred. When word got back to the high school, those who'd been at the bridge earlier knew who it was. The car was described as a blue Ford, the same car at which the arm had pointed three days earlier.

PARKE COUNTY

Soon after the 1809 Treaty of Fort Wayne opened portions of the state to settlement, pioneers entered the area via the Wabash River. Parke County was organized in 1821 and named for territorial congressman, judge and the first president of the Indiana Historical Society, Benjamin Parke.

The Wabash and Erie Canal, begun in 1832, reached the Parke County village of Coal Creek in 1847. Montezuma, on the western edge of the county, was platted in 1849 and named for the last Aztec emperor of Mexico; it was once an important canal town. A few traces remain of the canal and the basin, which was used to store and turn boats.

Although Parke County supports industry and agriculture, it is more often recognized for its turn-of-the-century villages and covered bridges. Of the fifty-seven covered bridges built in the county, more than half remain, many still in use. Some of them have stood for more than a century.

Within the boundaries of Parke County can be found three recreational areas: Shades State Park, which straddles the borders of Montgomery and Parke Counties, Raccoon Lake State Recreational Area and Turkey Run State Park. Turkey Run, established in 1916, is the second oldest Indiana State Park.

Bellmore—Dark Fantastic

The house was less than a mile west of Bellmore on US 36. Today it does not exist. The site stands empty. There may still be some older residents who remember hearing their grandparents tell the stories about the odd dwelling.

From the very start even the builders called it a crotchety house. The builders had troubles: the main chimney took far too long to erect because the bricks were mysteriously tumbling down during the night. Tools capriciously vanished during the day, turning up in unlikely places. These annoyances were not considered as anything but extraordinary aggravations until after the family moved in and began reporting sundry perplexing experiences, all suggestive of a diligent poltergeist. It was several years before the real clincher occurred.

Huge trees surrounded the house. One morning the family found, of all odd things to happen, that during the night much of their clothing had been evidently "sucked" out through the open windows and wrapped around trunks and branches of the trees.

As news of this event spread, people came to inspect the site and to offer explanations. Perhaps the clothes-whirling and tree-plastering had been done by some kind of a wind disturbance like a tornado. But how?

When the family had gone to bed the night had been still. The clothing was in trees on more than one side of the house, so the theory of a tornado didn't seem possible. Why hadn't there been any damage or other debris? Why did it touch only their home—their clothing—and nothing else?

The family decided it was a prank, not by a human, but by a ghost—a poltergeist! Several neighbors agreed with them. Even if someone had a ladder tall enough, which nobody in the vicinity did, some of the clothing was wrapped around branches too small to support the weight of a prankster unless he'd been a small primate.

It has been noted that poltergeists most frequently perform where young children live, and the family did have children.

Some of the clothing remained in the trees for several years until wind and weather wore them out. The house became a point of interest, attracting many curiosity seekers throughout the years and causing much speculation. But the mystery was never solved.

There were many other strange events that occurred at this house, but none so public as the family's shirts and pants decorating oaks and maples.

The strange happenings at the Bellmore home were the incentive for Margaret Echard's book, *The Dark Fantastic* (Doubleday & Company). Ms. Echard, an award-winning writer from Indiana, was the great-granddaughter of the family who had lived in and experienced the strange happenings in and around this house.

In the introduction to her book she wrote:

> *In my great-grandmother's house in Indiana, shortly after the close of the Civil War, a series of extraordinary events transpired which were never satisfactorily explained. The house was renowned for its hospitality and witnesses were not lacking to testify to the strange disturbances that in time became legend.*
>
> *Those disturbances are recorded in this novel as the subjective experience of one of the characters, and to that extent the work is founded on fact.*

❋❋❋

The Peek-A-Boo Ghost

Bill and Berky Davis have lived in their Parke County house for thirty-five years. George Walker had built the house in 1881 in an area called Walker's Bluff near Rosedale. The Davis' land abstract, which goes back to 1816, reads like who's who of early Indiana history. At one time there had been a cabin on the high bank of a section of the Wabash and Erie Canal. It's not known if the cabin had been there prior to the canal or if it had been constructed during the building of the canal to be used by the superintendent or a guard. The fact is, there's a lot of history and activity connected with the Davis lands and home.

One morning while Bill was shaving in the upstairs bathroom, looking in the mirror he caught sight of a little girl peeking around the corner of the bathroom door. When he turned around, she laughingly ran into the hallway.

Bill was home alone at the time. Naturally, he thought someone had come into the house and was teasing him. He put down his razor and quickly left the room in search of the little girl, calling to her, but never found her, though he searched throughout the house.

When his wife returned, he told her what had happened and asked her if she'd ever seen anything. Berky had never seen anything unusual.

This was not the last time Bill would see the little girl. The child seemed fond of Bill and enjoyed playing peek-a-boo with him. But one of their teenage daughters, whose bedroom was on the second floor, had also encountered her.

Bill has never seen her clearly, but he feels that she must be about six or seven, blond and wearing a blue dress. She's a happy and playful little ghost.

❋❋❋

Spook Light Hill

In a small farming community near Diamond on State Road 362, between Rosedale and Brazil, is an area called "Spook Light Hill." Here's the story behind the name.

One night the daughter of one of the farmers was driving home from her job in town. About two hundred yards from her home, as she began to drive up a small hill and across a narrow bridge, she apparently lost control and her car went off the bridge.

The police, fire department, her father and neighbors arrived at the tragic scene. After several minutes they were able to right the mangled car. Everyone hoped that somehow the girl had incredibly survived.

It was not to be. Evidently, the impact had thrown her into the windshield and nearly propelled her out of the automobile before it became airborne and began rolling over and over down the slight embankment. When the car was righted they found her partially out of the car—her shoulders and arms lying on the hood. She had been decapitated!

Police searched with flashlights in the dark, but were unable to find her head; they decided to wait until daylight to search further. The ambulance took her body back into town while the neighbors tried to comfort the grieving father.

The next day they and her father returned to search for the missing head, but never found it. They say she had a closed-coffin funeral and was buried without her head.

Her father became obsessed with finding the missing head and continued to seek it day and night. His neighbors said that often they would see his lantern light near that bridge. He lost interest in his farm and in day-to-day life; grief wrecked the man's health. After his death many forgot, or tried to forget, the horror of that night; however, some individuals, who have lived in this community for years, swear that from time-to-time they still see a light near that bridge gently swaying, much like a lantern.

Through the years people who scoffed at this story would go to the spot looking for the light and some have said they believed they had seen it. In 1969 a female college student from the area told the story of "Spook Light Hill" to one of her friends from Terre Haute. She told her that she and some other friends had gone to the bridge one night to see if they could see the light.

After they'd been there for a while and nothing had happened, they decided to leave and began to drive over the bridge—probably laughing and teasing each other—when someone spotted a light moving from beneath the bridge. They stopped and watched as it moved on up the slight incline and onto the road at the back of their car.

The reflection of the light similar to the dim light of the interior of the car, much like that of a lantern. They couldn't see anyone, or anything, holding the light! Slowly, following the road, it moved closer to the car. Finally, the students took off, certain that they had seen the old farmer—or at least the light from his lantern.

Through the years many stories have been told about "Spook Light Hill." Some tell of the auto accident, while others tell a story about a mining accident. (This is a coal mining area.) Then there are those who recall a murder committed by a jealous lover. All are certain, however, about the general location and that whatever horrible event took place had resulted in a decapitation and a grim, glowing light.

Tilghman's Furlough

One prominent Indiana family in Parke County did experience a ghostly visit almost a hundred and fifty years ago, and it has lived on in the local lore.

General Tilghman A. Howard was considered one of the greatest men from Parke County, a very popular Democrat who served as a state legislator in the 1830s. His political talents were recognized with his appointment to serve as minister to the Republic of Texas in 1844.

At the time, his supporters believed that he was sent there in order to get him out of the limelight because he was a too-likely candidate for the presidency of the United States.

Tilghman Howard's untimely death in Texas from yellow fever left his widow, Martha, with a family to rear in Rockville. They had two sons, Frank and young Tilghman. Both enlisted and fought during the Civil War, though in different regiments.

On September 1, 1862, Frank came home on furlough and spent the day visiting with friends and discussing the war. After he went to bed that night he found his upstairs room too hot for comfort and decided to sleep on the wooden bench in the downstairs hall. The family dog, a setter named Tanner, was overjoyed by the return of his young master and lay on the floor beside the bench.

Frank was sleeping soundly when the dog aroused him, howling. The young soldier reached down to soothe the dog and felt him crouched and trembling, with hackles raised. This was strange enough to fully awaken Frank. Sitting up he saw his brother, Tilghman standing in the moonlit open front door. He was delighted. Til, too, had come home on furlough! With a roar of joy Frank sprang up and ran to the door, but there was no one there.

After calling his brother's name a few times, he came back into the hall where Tanner still crouched in evident terror. Since the dog was devoted to both boys, Frank wondered why he had behaved in a menacing, terrified way.

The young men's mother was awakened by the commotion. He told her of his strange vision, an evident hallucination, and of the dog's remarkable behavior. Since Til was obviously not there, they dismissed it as a weird trick of moonlight and shadow.

Within a day or two official word was received that Captain Tilghman A. Howard Jr., aged twenty-two, had been killed at Uniontown, Kentucky.

Had Til come to say good-bye? In later years Frank Howard stated that he believed he'd seen his brother's ghost. (Precognition is a relatively common phenomenon, often during dreams.) Stating that if he alone had seen the specter he might've believed it was a dream. But Tanner was wide awake and the dog saw something terrifying.

❋❋❋

Turkey Run's Indian Under a Rock

By the 1840s there were few full-blooded Native Americans remaining in Parke County. One old Indian, nicknamed Johnny Green, still lived in the woods. He was harmless, except when he drank, said the old-timers. Then he could be unpredictable. County and regional stories of the time contain accounts of Native Americans who were left behind when their group had gone west. The tone of these stories is often patronizing and even scornful—when it should have been tragic.

Johnny roamed the woods and once in awhile would spend time at one of the farmer's homes—uninvited. The women were frightened by his presence because of pioneer stories of atrocities that the Indians inflicted on the early settlers. The last of these altercations had occurred during the War of 1812, so there had been many years between them and the time of the Johnny Green incident.

One chilly fall evening Johnny came to the home of Mr. Coleman Pruett. Mr. Pruett had gone to Rockville, leaving Mrs. Pruett alone. Hesitantly, Mrs. Pruett allowed Johnny Green into the house so he could sit by the fire and warm himself.

He began telling frightful tales of how the Indians had treated the settlers, making it quite clear that he'd enjoy nothing more than to repeat some of these horrors. Mrs. Pruett became frightened and insisted that he leave, which he did without incident.

When Mr. Pruett returned home his wife, in a very agitated and frightened state of mind, told him of the old Indian's visit.

According to the lore of the county, in fear for their family and angry at what seemed to be threatening behavior, the next day her husband and eldest son trailed the old Indian as far as Sugar Creek, where they camped for the night. The next day Mr. Pruett went alone and located Johnny Green fishing from Goose Rock just below the mouth of Turkey Run and shot him.

When his body fell it became trapped under the rock and it remained until time and the elements returned it to the earth.

Today, although, this area is a part of Turkey Run State Park, the exact location is not clear, according to park officials. Swimming in park waters has long been much discouraged because the current is treacherous and the water deep. Or is it because there are those who say they've seen the spirit of Johnny Green sitting on Goose Rock waiting to exact his revenge?

❋❋❋

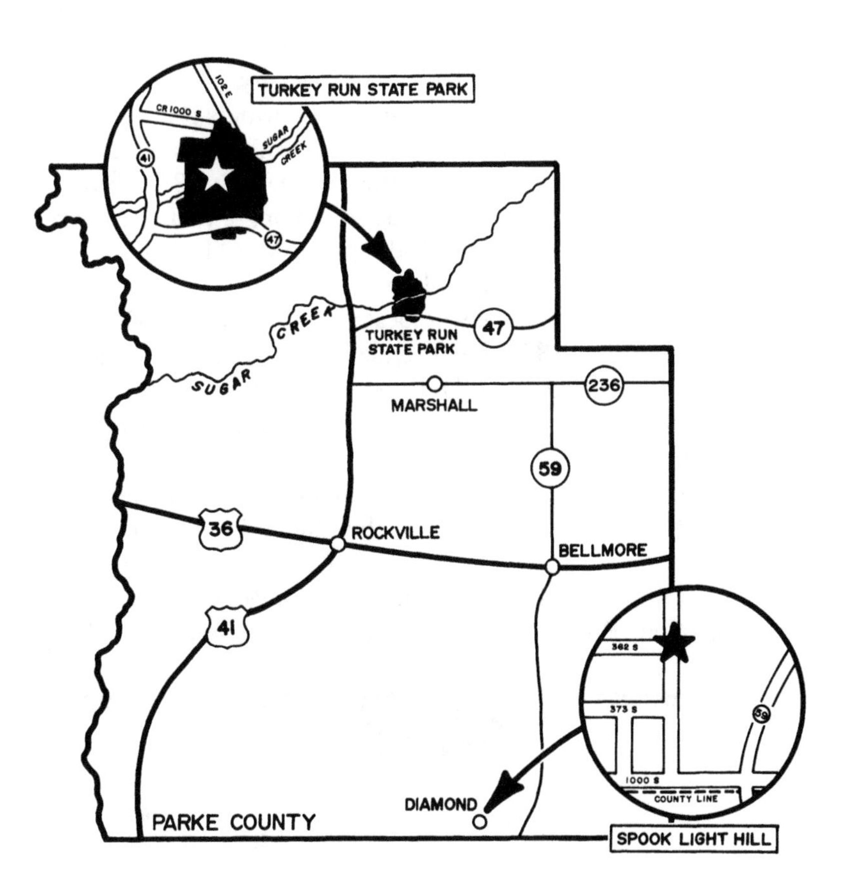

PUTNAM COUNTY

Putnam County was organized in 1822 and named for General Israel Putnam, an officer in the American Revolution. Putnam County is second only to Parke County in the number of covered bridges it has; most are located along Big Walnut Creek, which runs diagonally across the county. The southern part of the county borders the Richard Lieber State Recreation Area. The 8,075-acre area was established in 1952 and named in honor of Colonel Richard Lieber, who founded the state park system.

Most of the county's industries center on the county seat of Greencastle, conveniently located midway between Indianapolis and Terre Haute. It is the home of DePauw University.

The O'Hair family were prominent landowners prior to 1890, especially in an area known as Brick Chapel, which was established around and named for a church built there in the early 1830s. Several of the O'Hair brick homes can still be seen along a route following US 231 north from Greencastle. Today the J. M. O'Hair home is a private residence and an antique shop.

Eli Lilly's first drugstore was located in Greencastle, where the family had moved in 1852. He attended the preparatory school at Indiana Asbury College (now DePauw University). After the Civil War Lilly moved to Indianapolis where he founded the company which became a pharmaceutical giant.

Greencastle's Central National Bank gained notoriety when John Dillinger robbed it in 1933. Today the building is used for retail and office space.

Two of the county's oldest institutions—DePauw University and the Indiana State Penal Farm—provide continuing economic stability.

The Ghost of Governor Whitcomb

Every librarian's dream is to have a dedicated assistant who works whenever necessary, often late in the evening, asks for no paycheck and is 100 percent effective in encouraging borrowers to return overdue library books.

DePauw University had that perfect librarian . . . a ghost. The first report that a spectral being haunted old Whitcomb Library came in the early 1900s. Governor James Whitcomb had left his rare book collection to the school with the stipulation that they were never to be taken from the library building.

A student, however, found Whitcomb's favorite book, *The Poems of Ossian*, which had been given to the governor as a young boy, so interesting that he slipped it out of the building intending to read it that night and return it the next day. It was after midnight when he finished the book and turned the lights out.

He awoke with the sense that he was not alone. When his eyes became adjusted to the darkness, he saw a spectral finger pointing accusingly. And then he heard, "Who stole *Ossian*?" The bony hand reached toward the boy, who swore he felt a finger touch his cheek.

Governor Whitcomb had made his point. The boy returned the book stammering he'd been visited by the ghost of Governor Whitcomb and promising he'd never take another restricted book out of the library.

Today, the books are housed in a new building in a secure area where only librarians can retrieve the rare volumes.

Locust Hill

Six miles north of Greencastle on US 231 sits the two-story brick O'Hair house. Built in 1834, it was the home of Mr. and Mrs. J. M. O'Hair and their eleven children for many years.

The house sat empty for several years until Mr. and Mrs. David C. Arnold purchased it in 1986 and began restoration. Today the house is known as Locust Hill and functions as an antique shop, an art gallery and the home of the proprietors.

During the years they've owned the venerable house, the Arnolds and one of their sons admit to experiencing events that cannot be logically explained. Among these strange incidents are doors slamming shut by themselves, water turning on by itself in the upstairs bathroom, the sound of music and the coughing of a deep voiced man.

These are all associated with the interior or living space of the house.

The Arnolds also report hearing sounds coming from outside of the house that can only be described as the jingling of horse harnesses followed by the sound of talking and laughter—sounds announcing the arrival of spirit guests from the past.

Dave Arnold remembers how helpful the "others" can be. One day, alone in the house, he was working on the plumbing and was having trouble getting one of the pipes to come loose. The telephone rang just as he was beginning to lose his temper.

He left the room to answer the call and take a break. When he returned he found the pipe had been removed and was lying on the floor. He quietly thanked his spectral plumber's helper.

The mysterious sounds of music and a man's voice fill the O'Hair house, while the jingling sounds of horse harnesses can be heard approaching.

Photo by David C. Arnold

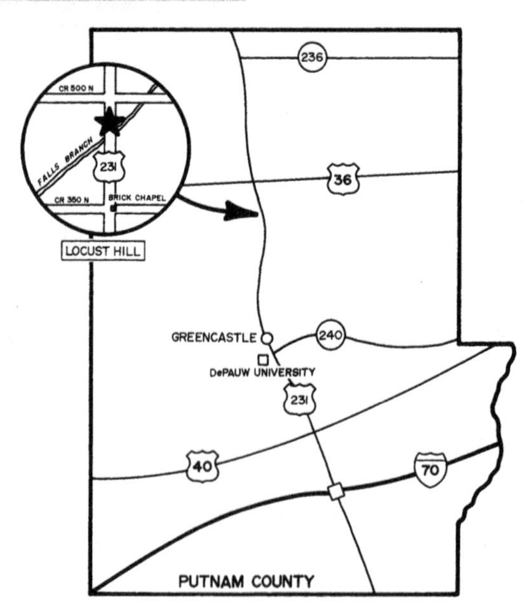

VIGO COUNTY

Vigo County was organized in 1818 and named for Colonel Francis Vigo, a Sardinian merchant-trader who came to Vincennes about 1777. He supplied George Rogers Clark with information, money and materials during the Revolutionary War to aid in ending British dominance.

The county seat was originally a French settlement from about 1720 to 1763 and was called Terre Haute, French for "high land." Fort Harrison was constructed in 1811 near the site of a Wea village.

Terre Haute's economic development prior to 1860 hinged on the evolution of a transportation system encompassing river, highway, canal and railroad. The first steamboat, *Florence*, docked at Terre Haute about 1823. Soon a stream of packets, flatboats, barges and other river craft transporting farm produce and passengers crowded the riverfront. The National Road, the major east-west thoroughfare, reached the city in 1835. Next came the Wabash and Erie Canal in 1849, closely followed by the railroads.

Education became an important part of the community's development, with school buildings appearing on the average of one every two years, including St. Mary-of-the-Woods, Indiana State Normal School (now Indiana State University) and Rose Polytechnic Institute (today's Rose-Hulman Institute of Technology).

Socialist Eugene V. Debs was one of a number of prominent persons with connections to Terre Haute. His house is on the corner of Sycamore and 8th Streets and is open to the public Wednesday through Sunday from 1:00 to 4:30 PM. (Ring the doorbell on Wednesdays.)

The city's contributors to the arts included songwriter Paul Dresser, who wrote "On the Banks of the Wabash Far Away," and Theodore Dreiser, Paul's brother and acclaimed novelist.

The Blue Hole

Following Highway 63 for about eight miles south of Terre Haute is the town of Prairieton and a legendary lake, the three-acre, so-called bottomless Blue Hole.

Stories have been told of a prehistoric water monster who lives in the depths of the Blue Hole—a Hoosier Loch Ness Monster. There are those who claim that the monster is in actuality a huge catfish, its head the size of a rain barrel.

All along the Wabash River pirates were very active during Indiana's early years. Numerous stories are told of their evidently lucrative and often deadly exploits. Somewhere in the vicinity of the Blue Hole, it's rumored that pirates buried their treasure. At least one other pirate treasure story tells of an unnamed pirate who buried his treasure at the bottom of Blue Hole and set up a series of traps to protect the treasure. Thus far, no one has been able to unearth a single gold coin.

Six cabins used to sit around the lake, supposedly built and used as hide-outs for Chicago gangsters. A few believe that while the gangsters were in residence, they did more than fish at the lake. They'd tie a heavy rock around the ankle—or necks—of victims and toss them into the lake.

Many people in the area believe that a force in the middle of the lake will suck an individual or an item into an underground river that eventually flows into the Wabash River. Others believe the bottom is quicksand.

One of the tall tales told about the Blue Hole involves the disappearance of a bus full of children. The bus was crossing the bridge over the Blue Hole when the driver lost control, plunging the bus into the water. Neither the bus nor children were ever found. History does not support the claims of such terrible events.

Another tale is about a train jumping the track as it crosses the Blue Hole bridge and plunging into the water. No sign of the train was ever found.

Still the persistent telling of these tall tales added to the belief that the Blue Hole was bottomless.

Some years ago, a group of teenage boys went swimming in the Blue Hole. When the boys did not return the parents became concerned and looked for them. When they reached the hole they found the boys' clothing on the bank, but never found the boys. Word went around that they'd been sucked into the vortex and drowned.

In 1969 two curious officers from the Vigo County Sheriff's Department spent a day under the waters of the Blue Hole. They were looking to either refute or substantiate some of the legends surrounding the water. They didn't find any sign of a train or a bus. They did, however, feel a pull near the bottom as if there was an underground stream. They estimated the maximum depths at between twenty-two and thirty feet.

From time to time stories of ghosts surface from the depths of the Blue Hole. The victims of gangland violence, the lost and drowned children, the train crew all appear to the unwary as a warning of what tragedy may await them if they enter the bottomless Blue Hole.

There are other famous bottomless Blue Holes located in Indiana, one located in Daviess County just west of Washington near the west fork of White River, another in Jackson County near Seymour along the east fork of White River.

The Ultimate Long Distance Call

Blue skies, white clouds and the summer sun shining on neat homes with shrubs, trees and brightly blooming flowerbeds. Children laughing and playing, dogs barking, the sounds of lawnmowers and a neighbor's hand raised as he calls out a friendly greeting to the postman. This was a typical Terre Haute neighborhood of the 1920s.

The people who lived here had seen it all. They'd lived through World War I, weathered recession, Prohibition and "the New Woman" with bobbed hair and short skirts.

This was a Norman Rockwell neighborhood with ordinary normal neighbors, with one exception, Martin Sheets.

Many of his neighbors knew Martin was an eccentric and left him alone to do things his own way. However, they didn't realize that he could be volatile and even dangerous. The owner of a garage next door would occasionally park a car in front of his home. On one occasion, Sheets lay waiting in his own car while his neighbor proceeded to park a car in the front of the house. Putting it into drive, Sheets gunned the engine and rammed the other car. He then jumped out and threatened the man with a gun. The confrontation ended in a volley of angry words.

No one was surprised when Sheets devised a bizarre plan for himself after his death. Sheets had been born before the turn of the century, a time when many still believed it was possible for a person to be buried alive. Stories were common of individuals thought to be dead but actually in a state of comatose suspension, awakening to the horror of a slow suffocating death underground. Edgar Allen Poe had, of course, stimulated these beliefs with his stories of cataleptic fits that slowed metabolism to the point where the non-dead would be mistakenly buried.

Sheets wanted to make sure that this did not happen to him. Instead, sixteen years before his death, he had a large mausoleum erected in Terre Haute's Highland Lawn Cemetery for himself and his wife. This in itself was not eccentric. However, word got out that he'd ordered a casket to be built with special latches enabling it to be opened from the INSIDE.

The whole town began talking about his final precaution. Nat Crawford, manager of the Indiana Bell Telephone Company, had told one of his superintendents that Martin Sheets had just signed an order to have a telephone installed in his mausoleum!

There was some difficulty in deciding how to run the line to the mausoleum. Should it be overhead or underground? There were no poles in the cemetery. Eventually the decision was made to install the line above ground.

Sheets' will stipulated that this telephone was to remain in operating condition in perpetuity. It also stated that a rocking chair and a bottle of whiskey were to be placed in his tomb at the time of his demise. In the event that he would find himself in the situation he most wanted to avoid—being buried alive—he could open the casket and call someone to come and get him out of the mausoleum. Meanwhile he would wait for them in his rocking chair sipping whiskey.

On February 27, 1926, Martin Sheets died and was interred in his mausoleum along with the telephone, rocking chair and a bottle of whiskey.

After several years his wife, Susan, passed away. She had been found with the telephone receiver in her hand dead of a heart attack. Rumors circulated that she had died of sheer fright. This rumor was strengthened when the mausoleum was opened to receive her body and it was found that the telephone receiver was off the hook.

Years later, since the telephone maintenance had been in Sheets' will, the cemetery's board of regents had to petition the court for permission to have the telephone removed from the mausoleum. It is no longer there. At the time of its removal the rocking chair and bottle of whiskey were also gone.

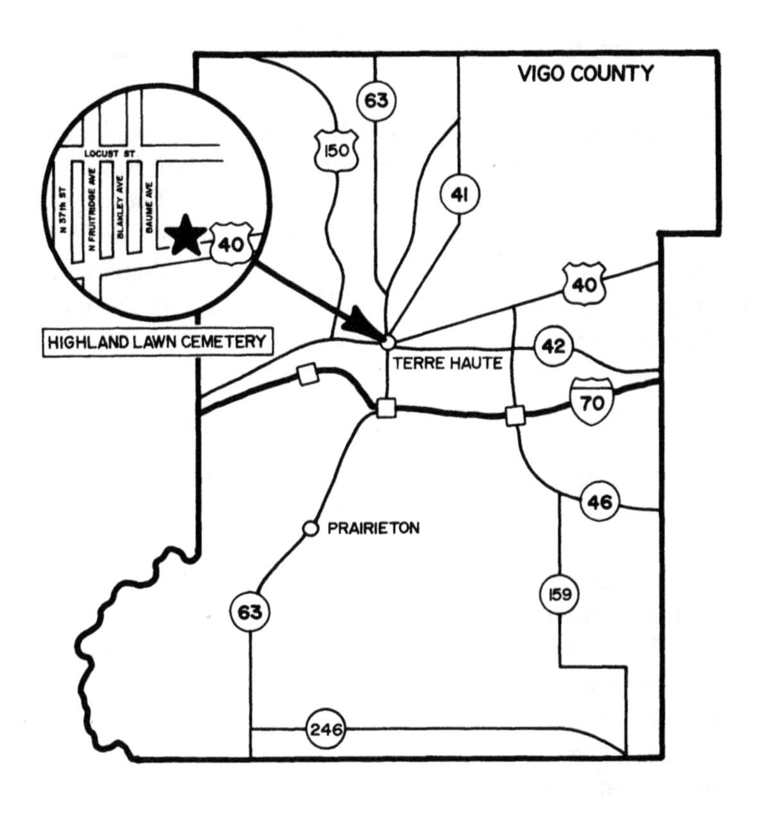
VIGO COUNTY
LOCUST ST
N 37th ST
N FRUITRIDGE AVE
BLAKLEY AVE
BAUME AVE
40
HIGHLAND LAWN CEMETERY
63
150
41
40
42
TERRE HAUTE
70
46
PRAIRIETON
63
159
246

WARREN COUNTY

This county was organized in 1827 and named for Major General Joseph Warren, the Massachusetts physician and Revolutionary War soldier who was killed at Breed's Hill in 1775. The state of Illinois creates the county boundary to the west. Tippecanoe County is to the east, and Benton County to the north. The Wabash River is the county's southern boundary line. Warren is primarily an agricultural county with some mining and industry.

From the 1890s to the 1940s, a luxurious mineral springs spa called Mudlavia Hotel operated north of the Fountain County town of Attica; it attracted the rich and famous from near and far. Several of these notables would stay at the Attica Hotel for one of their famous steak dinners before proceeding the next day to Mudlavia.

Williamsport was platted and established as the county seat in 1828 and named for William Harrison, the owner of a tavern and ferry across the Wabash. A side-cut canal was constructed between 1850 and 1852 to enable boats to run to the west side of the river.

Williamsport Falls is the county's most widely known natural landmark. From an overhanging ledge it drops a distance of 67 feet into a rocky ravine. The water's fall varies from a trickle in the dry summer months to a spectacular torrent during spring thaws.

Harrison's Phantom Militia

By late 1811 the number of settlers in Indiana and eastern Illinois had steadily increased. The land was being stripped of its virgin wilderness and replaced by farms and settlements. The Indians sought to stop the white man from taking their land, and under the leadership of Tecumseh they terrorized the settlers up and down the length of the Wabash River. Tecumseh decided the only way to stop white man's encroachment into Indian lands was to form a confederation of midwestern, southern and some western Indians.

On September 12, 1811, William Henry Harrison's militia marched toward Vincennes, where it remained for one week. Once again the 1000-men militia, comprised of U.S. regulars and volunteers such as the Corydon Yellow Jackets, began marching north to a place on the Wabash River at Williamsport, just above present day Terre Haute. At that site they erected a stockade, Fort Harrison, in an effort to secure the Wabash Valley against Tecumseh's threats.

The first week of November they left the fort and continued toward the Indian village known as Prophet's Town, near present-day Battle Ground, where they planned to camp and negotiate with the Indians. Nearing the village they were met by a messenger carrying a white flag and the message that a delegation wanted to talk to Harrison. The delegation, which assured Harrison it desired peace, promised to meet the general the next day to settle the terms of peace.

Though the village contained many women and children, a fact that should have indicated the Indians were not planning to wage war, Harrison was suspicious. The men were given precautionary orders to sleep on their rifles that night.

Around four the next morning the men awoke to the sound of gunfire. The battle began. When it was over the militia casualties totaled 108, including sixty-two dead. Thirty-six Indian bodies along with numerous fresh graves were found on the battlefield. Harrison's militia had won the battle. It marked the virtual end of the idea of Indian confederation in the Midwest.

The battle, however, may not be over for Harrison's militia. For several decades, the occupants of a two-story frame house twelve miles north of Williamsport have experienced a strange occurrence.

It's believed that the house in question is on the route General Harrison and his militiamen took on their way to the Battle of Tippecanoe. On certain nights in early November the unmistakable sound of marching feet approaching from a southerly direction can be heard. The ghostly sounds of marching men grow louder as they near the house and then gradually recede as they pass to the northeast. There have been no sightings of the militia, only echoes from the past, as the spectral troops presumably move on to engage the spirits of dead Shawnee, Miami and Sauk Fox at the haunted site of one of the decisive battles in American history.

WAYNE COUNTY

The territorial legislature carved Wayne County from northern Dearborn County in 1811 and named it for General Anthony Wayne, officer in the Revolution but noted here mainly for his defeat of Little Turtle at the Battle of Fallen Timbers in 1794.

The county seat, Richmond, the "Queen City of the Whitewater Valley," was platted in 1816 and originally named Smithville, for the proprietor John Smith. An adjoining town was laid out in 1818 by Jeremiah Cox and called Coxborough. In 1818 the two towns were incorporated together as Richmond. The name was selected for the commendatory idea of richness of soil.

Richmond's first newspaper, the *Richmond Palladium*, founded in 1831 by Nelson Boon, grand-nephew of Daniel Boone, is one of the three oldest Indiana newspapers and Richmond's oldest surviving business. The newspaper's fourth editor and Richmond's mayor from 1852 to 1866, John Finley, is credited with popularizing the term "Hoosier" through his poem "The Hoosier's Nest" that first appeared in the January 1, 1833 *Indianapolis Journal.*

Earlham College, founded in 1847, was opened as the Friends' Boarding School and became Earlham College in 1859 when it added a collegiate department and began granting degrees. Earlham was named for Earlham Hall, the ancestral home of the Gurney family, well-known Quakers of Norwich, England.

Cry-Woman Bridge

The town of Dublin is located in east central Indiana on US 40. Just southeast of Dublin on Heacock Road, a typical twisting country road, was a bridge once known to the local residents as Cry-Woman Bridge.

Late one rainy night a young mother and her baby, newcomers to the county, were driving back to her home when she lost control of her car at a sharp curve just before the bridge entrance. The car plunged into the rain-swollen creek.

Searchers later found her body. However, the only sign of the baby was a muddy, rain-soaked blanket. The authorities tried to locate relatives, but no one came to claim her body. The county buried the woman in a pauper's grave, with, so the story goes, her baby's blanket beside her.

After the incident people began "seeing" the ghost of a woman near the bridge, particularly on foggy or rainy nights. Those who said they had seen her also reported hearing her sobbing and pitifully crying out, "Where is my baby?"

Most individuals in the area would not tarry near the bridge; however, just before it was replaced, a young couple decided to tempt fate and see if there really was a ghost haunting the site of the accident. One night they parked near the bridge. They didn't have long to wait before the woman appeared.

They heard the heart-stopping sobs and then they heard her pleading call, "Baby, where have you gone? Baby, baby where are you?" After the initial paralyzing fright, they started the car and left the Cry-Woman Bridge behind them.

Does she still search for her baby? There haven't been any recent reports of encounters, although most everyone in the community is familiar with the story and the site. Perhaps they're just not talking.

Southern Indiana

BARTHOLOMEW COUNTY

Created in 1821 from a section of what had been Delaware County, Bartholomew was named for General Joseph Bartholomew, one of the county's organizers who had been a hero at the Battle of Tippecanoe.

General John Tipton (1786–1839) purchased several hundred acres in 1820, and a county seat, eventually named Columbus, began to be populated.

Settlers, mostly from Kentucky, Virginia and the Carolinas, began settling in the new town; however, its growth was slow due to the swampy and malaria-infested environs. As well as overcoming the rough terrain, settlers had to fight off wild animals and crop-destroying pests.

Grist, saw and woolen mills along with distilleries were established along the main streams, utilizing the abundant waterpower to process the produce of the county. The agricultural surplus was loaded on flatboats and floated to markets as far south as New Orleans. Hogs were driven on foot over state roads to the pork-packing houses in Madison.

The most encouraging development in stabilizing the county's unpredictable economy came in the early and mid-twentieth century when heavy industries moved into the area. These included Cummins Diesel Engines, founded by Clessie Cummins and W. G. Irwin in 1919; Arvin Industries, founded by Q. C. Noblitt and Frank Sparks in 1927; and Cosco, Inc., founded by B. F. Hamilton and Sons in 1935.

Today the county's economy is based on farming, industry, and tourism. Columbus has become a center of admirable architecture, fine arts and civic pride.

The Azalia Bridge

The village of Azalia, platted in 1831 and believed to be named for the flower, is a short distance south of Columbus on US 31. According to local lore the founders had hoped the community would be pure and undefiled, a model of temperance in all aspects.

Unfortunately a young unmarried girl in the community did not live up to the dreams of the founders. She became pregnant, but was able to conceal her sin until spring when the baby was born. Shunned by both her family and the community, she and the baby left the village.

No one knows where she and the baby stayed. Some farmers said they saw them around decaying, abandoned barns. Afraid to enter the town or seek aid from her family, she would scavenge and even steal food to survive.

She must have gone insane. What else could explain what she did with her tiny baby? Not too far from town is a bridge spanning Sand Creek. Normally, the water would be little more than ankle deep. However, with the melting snow and spring freshets, the creek was running fast and deep with icy cold water. The crazed young mother, holding her baby wrapped in a thin white blanket, stood on the bridge watching the wild currents rushing past. Leaning over the edge, she opened her arms and let the baby fall; she watched as the current carried the bundle away until it was out of sight.

Sometime later a fisherman found the remains of the baby still wrapped securely in its blanket. The haggard mother, wild-eyed, ranting, moaning and crying, was left alone, as was the custom of early-nineteenth-century villages, to wander the countryside and repent. She continued to forage and steal food and found shelter wherever she could. This was a far worse sentence than any court of law could have given her.

For many years she lurked around the creek bed and sat at the foot of the bridge, rocking and wailing. Those who saw her, though frightened, believed she was truly sorry and mourned for the child she had killed.

One day she was seen sitting on the bank, but unlike other times she was not rocking and was silent. She was dead. No one knows who buried her or where.

There are those who say if you go to the Azalia Bridge and dare to look over you might see the baby, wrapped tightly in a white blanket, lying at the edge of the water crying for its mother. Wait long enough and you'll get a glimpse of the desperate, insane mother and hear her mournful crying.

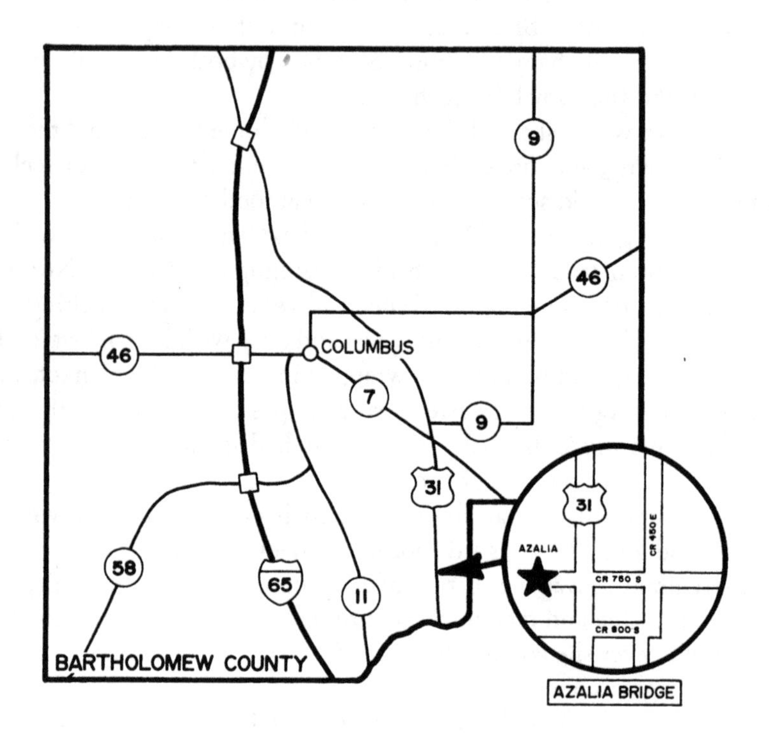
9
46
46
COLUMBUS
7
9
31
58
65
11
BARTHOLOMEW COUNTY
31
AZALIA
CR 450 E
CR 760 S
CR 800 S
AZALIA BRIDGE

BROWN COUNTY

Organized in 1836, the county was named for Major General Jacob J. Brown, known for his heroic combat during the War of 1812. He later became a commanding officer from 1821 to 1828 of the United States Army.

Most of the county is too hilly to support agriculture, so methods of obtaining natural resources such as timber, salt and gold were developed. Glaciers were said to have deposited large amounts of gold in the area's hills; therefore, in 1875 settlers concentrated much of their efforts on gold mining. The unsuccessful industry closed after approximately fifty years.

The scenic area at the county line once was known as Stoney Lonesome because rough terrain and underbrush made travel through the region treacherous. Compounding the danger were bands of robbers who would ambush settlers or salesmen as they made their way between Columbus and Nashville. The White Caps, an independent secret organization similar to the Ku Klux Klan, dominated the area and local government from the 1880s until the turn of the century.

The village of Story, located at the crossroads of 135 and the Elkinsville Road, once known as Storyville, was named for one of the first settlers in the area, Dr. Story. The village became the economic and social hub for several small, isolated villages, including Elkinsville, which was founded in 1850 and named for the first settler, William Elkins.

Artists have long frequented Brown County. The T. C. Steele studio and home preserves the flavor of the artist colonies of the 1920s.

Since the 1930s the county's economy has developed a reliance on the tourist trade. Many of the residents commute to jobs in Bloomington, Columbus or Indianapolis.

The Haunting of Story, Indiana

Employees and several guests at the Story Inn on State Road 135 know the room at the top of the stairs as the "Blue Lady" room, so named for a spectral visitor who evidently has made it her permanent residence. She's been seen standing at the edge of the bed, reflected in the window or the mirror.

One worker who has been employed by the inn for more than ten years saw a metal coffeepot fall off of a cabinet with no one near. She has also seen another ghost in the inn. On her way downstairs to take a call she saw a cream-colored skirt swoosh around a corner. When she reached the bottom of the stairs no one was in sight. There was no other way out.

A picture of an old lady dressed in dark, nineteenth-century clothing hangs on the wall behind the service desk. It seems to have a "life" of it's own. One of the owners commented to an employee, "She sure wasn't very pretty." Suddenly the picture crashed to the floor. The nail was firmly in the wall and the wire was intact!

Encounters continue to be reported. The aroma of cherry tobacco often accompanies sightings of the Blue Lady dressed in a floor length gown. Though no one knows who the Blue Lady is, the employees have decided she must be one of Dr. Story's wives, though there's no reason to believe this.

The inn isn't the only haunted building in Story. Dr. George Story, the town's founder, built his home on the highest point in the town. Visitors and employees believe his house is haunted. On more than one occasion the housekeeper has been pinched as she cleans the house. She's also reported lights on in rooms after she's turned them off and doors opening and closing without anyone being near them.

The Story Inn. The "Blue Lady" shares the bedroom at the top of the stairs with the inn's guests and is often credited with trips and tricks.

Photo by Wanda L. Willis

Odd occurrences have been known to happen at Dr. Story's house. Visitors and employees are convinced it's haunted. But by whom?

Photo by Eric Mundell

❋❋❋

Attorney Rick Hofstetter and his partner, chef Frank Mueller, purchased twenty-five acres of the village of Story, creating a bed and breakfast community.

Rick is a college chum of my friend, Nelson Price. In May 2001, Nelson, an author, Logan Ericson, an historian, and I spent a weekend at Rick's Story Inn.

I was booked in the haunted "Blue Lady" room, while the others were settled into rooms at the other end of the inn. Just for fun I'd brought my ouija board and a white candle of purity and innocence. After dinner the three of us planned to "contact" the lady.

After arriving, the three of us went our separate ways. Nelson went to his room to write. Logan went into the herb garden to read, and I remained in my room relaxing until we were to go to dinner.

Since my room was at the top of the stairs we decided I'd wait for my friends to come by before going downstairs. I was looking out my bedroom window while waiting for my friends when I felt a presence behind me. I turned to find I was alone. Had the "Blue Lady" paid me a visit?

That evening at dinner I sat across from my friends and directly in front of Logan. The waitress arrived to take our orders and at that precise moment Logan's Merlot was thrown in my face! Red wine dripped from my hair, into my eyes, down my chin and neck. Silent and stunned we sat there while the waitress was frozen in disbelief. No one had touched the wine glass.

Later we went to my room—the Blue Lady's room—lit the candle, and turned out the lights. Sitting on the floor between the mirror, bed and window, where she'd often been sighted, we placed our fingertips lightly on the planchette and began beseeching her to communicate.

"Are you here with us?" Then—slowly—the pointer began to move—stopping at "H" and then "I"! Nelson, a true non-believer, asked, "Wanda, did you do that?" How could I? All three of us had our fingers resting on the lozenge.

It became apparent that she more readily responded to Logan, so Nelson and I became silent observers. Logan sat with his eyes shut and fingers on the pointer and asked her to "Give us a sign." We watched as once again the word "Hi" was spelled out. Gently Logan urged the lady to tell us her name. The indicator began to move pointing to "S—T." At the edge of the mirror a milky blue haze began to appear and then it was gone. All contact between her and Logan stopped. None of us "believed" what we had experienced, not really, and yet . . . Even our skeptical friend, Nelson, admitted something had happened. We all decided that the ST had to be the beginning of the name STORY!

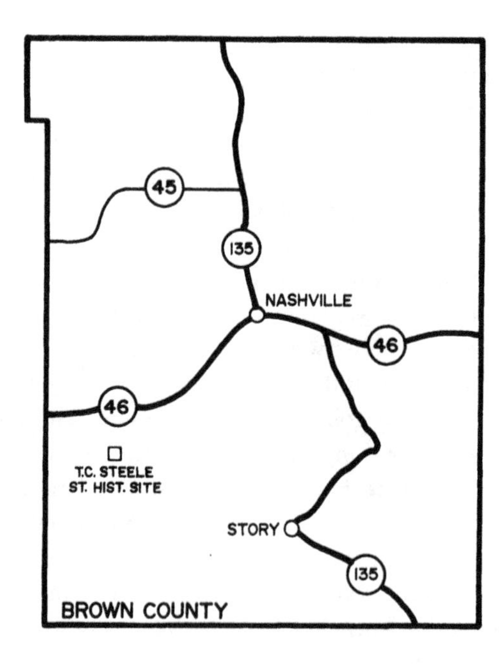

DEARBORN COUNTY

Dearborn County, the state's third-oldest county, was formed in 1803 and named for Major General Henry Dearborn, who at the time was secretary of war under President Thomas Jefferson.

Lawrenceburg, the county seat, is Indiana's fourth oldest city and Dearborn County's largest community.

Lawrenceburg's Eads Parkway and Park were named after an important early Lawrenceburg citizen, James Buchanan Eads (1820–1887), an engineer and inventor, who gained a fortune in the river salvage business; he invented and patented the first diving bell in 1842. During the Civil War, he was commissioned by Abraham Lincoln to construct fourteen armored boats and other river craft. He is best known for the Eads Bridge built between 1867 and 1874, which spans the Mississippi River at St. Louis.

Two memorials in the park are a bell in memory of Lawrenceburg firemen and a marker commemorating the city's two governors, Albert Gallatin Porter (1824–1897) and Winfield Taylor Durbin (1847-1928), the fourteenth and eighteenth governors of Indiana respectively.

A section of the Whitewater Canal from Lawrenceburg to West Harrison in the northeast corner of the county was completed in 1839. The turning basin extended from the foot of Elm Street, two blocks northeast of Walnut Street, to the foot of St. Clair Street.

One of America's most celebrated clergymen of the nineteenth century, Henry Ward Beecher, began his ministry at age twenty-three in 1837 at the Lawrenceburg First Presbyterian Church (renamed in 1922 Beecher Presbyterian Church). Two years later he accepted another position with the Second Presbyterian Church in Indianapolis.

Moores Hill Male and Female Collegiate Institute, 1854, was the second Indiana college to adopt coeducation. Today the institution still exists in Vanderburg County as the University of Evansville.

Aurora, eleven miles east of Moores Hill on Route 350, overlooks the picturesque bend of the Ohio River. The city was founded in 1819 and named by Indiana Supreme Court Justice Jesse Holman.

The Laughery Creek Road Massacre

Fire destroys both animate and inanimate objects, but it cannot destroy the ghosts of the past reported to be haunting Dearborn County's Laughery Creek Road.

As the summer home of an Indianapolis family burned in August 1970, the community began remembering the horrible crime committed there twenty-nine years earlier, at which time the Johnston Agrue family was in residence, having owned the farm for nearly twenty-five years. They were an industrious, well-liked, large family that included six daughters, all of whom had married and left home, and two sons, Leo, twenty-two, and William, thirty-three, who still lived with their parents on the family farm.

On a Saturday morning in May 1941, their neighbor, Harvey Sellers, had come to the Agrue farm to inform the family that their cows were in his alfalfa field. As he was proceeding toward the house he came across the body of Johnston Agrue. Believing that he'd committed suicide, Mr. Sellers hurried to the farm and was startled at the sight of the body of the Agrues' eleven-year-old granddaughter just inside the barn door. He then made his way to the Joseph Schmidt farm, the nearest one that had a telephone, and called the sheriff.

When the group of law enforcement officers arrived at the farm they decided to toss a teargas bomb into the farmhouse in case the killer was hiding inside. When the air cleared they entered the house to find Mrs. Agrue dead on the kitchen floor in a pool of blood.

After they searched the grounds, the body of Leo Agrue was found on the hillside where he and his brother, William, had been planting corn. William was nowhere to be found on the farm. Assuming he was the killer, an armed posse began searching the surrounding area.

He was found near the Wilson School House—dead—shot in the back as he apparently tried to run away from the assailant.

Who could have committed this horrible crime and why? Members of the family were questioned. From the first, suspicion was directed toward a son-in-law who had twice married into the family. There had been bad feelings between him and the family. He was taken into custody for questioning and then taken to Indianapolis where he was given a lie detector test and confessed to the frightful crime.

Under armed guard he was taken to the scene of the crime and led the police to an old hollow tree where he'd hidden the shotgun used to murder the five members of the Agrue family.

After many delays the son-in-law was brought to trial. He was sentenced to death in the electric chair, a sentence that was carried out in Michigan City in February 1942.

Nothing is left of the Agrues' home, which burned to the ground in August 1970. The memory of the gruesome crime still haunts the community, but that's not all. Laughery Creek Road (following the creek), which marks the boundary between Delaware and Ohio County, is a typical lonely country back road. Many swear that it's haunted. Driving the road is an extremely uncomfortable experience for many, and although there have been no sightings or encounters, many feel a sense of dark foreboding.

Is the son-in-law's evil spirit still stalking the Agrue family? Or, are the spirits of the Agrues waiting to take their revenge on the son-in-law?

❋❋❋

FLOYD COUNTY

Floyd County is believed to have been named for Colonel Davis Floyd, who was killed by Indians on the Kentucky side of the Ohio River. Floyd's association with Aaron Burr's conspiracy to embroil America in a war with Spain in 1807 earned him time in jail, a small fine, and the distinction of being the only Burr co-conspirator tried and convicted. Just days after his sentencing, Indiana's territorial legislature elected him clerk of the lower house.

Founded in 1813, New Albany, named for the capital of New York State, was Indiana's most populous city from the 1830s into the 1850s. Positioned in the lowland east of a steep slope called the Knobstone Escarpment, between the city and the steepest part of the escarpment, is a group of hills known as the Knobs, which forms a scenic backdrop and city overlook. New Albany, Jeffersonville, Clarksville and Louisville are known as the Falls Cities, so designated because they are located at the falls of the Ohio River.

One of New Albany's citizens, Ashbel P. Willard, a local attorney and former lieutenant governor became governor in 1856. He died three months before his term ended, the first Indiana governor to die in office.

Another famous Floyd County citizen was Sherman Minton, who was born in neighboring Georgetown, educated in New Albany schools, and appointed to the United State Supreme Court by President Harry S. Truman in 1949. In 1951 Georgetown was again highlighted when its native son R. Carlyle Buley was awarded the Pulitzer Prize in history for his two-volume series, *The Old Northwest,* which chronicled the historical development of that area.

Blue Balls of Light

In the first half of the nineteenth century, Captain Francis T. McHarry, an Irish immigrant from Louisville, ran a ferry between Louisville and New Albany. During the canal-building frenzy, he invested in the privately owned Portland Canal venture. It was awarded the first contract for the proposed canal around the Falls of the Ohio.

In 1843 Captain McHarry purchased a riverboat built at the Howard Shipyards in Jeffersonville and christened it the *Music*. One day a violent fight erupted onboard, and when the captain intervened he was mortally wounded. For several days he lay waiting for his inevitable fate. During this time he gave precise instructions for his burial. Oddly, he told those at his deathbed watch that he was to be buried upright, in a hilltop tomb overlooking the Ohio River. On February 15, 1857, he died.

His limestone mausoleum, built into a limestone cliff, stands over four hundred feet above the Ohio, eleven miles east from New Albany. It was erected on Beeler Hill—today known as Vault Point Knob—a privately owned and inaccessible location.

It is possible that some of the Irish who worked on the Portland Canal built the impressive structure. When completed it was forty feet long by twenty feet high. A porthole was installed above the door, from which, presumably, McHarry's ghost could keep an eye on the river.

Part of the story is that, being a good Irishman, McHarry also requested his body be placed in a barrel of whiskey; however, the laborers could not bear the thought of good whiskey being wasted and drained the barrel before the captain could be put in it. McHarry's wife had no desire whatsoever to spend eternity in a lonely, strange tomb high above the Ohio River. When she died her husband's body was exhumed and reburied beside her in the Irwin Mausoleum at Cave Hill Cemetery in Louisville.

This is not the end of his story, however. McHarry had evidently become angry over some dealings with other riverboat captains and vowed, before he died, he'd curse them throughout eternity. McHarry's ghost is said to hurl curses from his tomb toward Ohio riverboat captains. For years, it was tradition for steamboats passing under his mausoleum to toot their whistles as a sign of respect and to ward off the curse.

According to the legend, during certain phases of the moon or on foggy nights glimpses of the ghost can be seen. At other times a shrill scream is said to come down from the tomb when steamboats pass during the night. Several captains in the past swore they saw blue balls of light and swirls of white mist emanating from his tomb. They believed, and some may still believe, that McHarry is still there in spirit, watching over the river that was responsible for both his wealth and his death.

McHARRY'S TOMB

High on the cleft where the wild birds soar,
and the eagle has her eyrie,
in a niche of the rock in walled with stone,
is the lonely grave of McHarry.
No hunter's horn or boatman's song,
nor stormy winds so dreary,
that whistles and raves around that grave,
will disturb the repose of McHarry.

Far away from his native land he sleeps
on the banks of our beautiful river,
whilst blue skies above, bright emblems of hope,
over his sepulchre hover.

And every traveler that passes the way,
and has but a moment to tarry,
will point to the cleft, to the tomb in the rock,
of the true, the lamented McHarry.

[Unknown]

(*Daily Ledger Standard;* April 25, 1872)

Captain Francis T. McHarry, a ferry captain on the Ohio River and investor in the Portland Canal venture became angry with other riverboat captains and vowed he'd curse them throughout eternity. McHarry's ghost is said to hurl curses from his tomb built on an inaccessible cliff over four hundred feet above the Ohio.

Photo by Ben Schneider

The Ghosts of Culbertson Mansion

Things that go bump in the dark, slamming doors, thumping noises in far-off rooms, vacuum cleaners starting by themselves, and other weird happenings abound in the 1869 New Albany Culbertson Mansion at 914 E. Main Street. Not all the hauntings involve spooky sounds. There have been sightings of a gray-haired ghost lingering in rooms and halls.

Ever since the state acquired the property in 1976, the staff have reported many strange experiences: dimmed lights, weird whispering in dark hallways, footsteps echoing and items disappearing. The employees find encounters with the spirit world more annoying than frightening.

Though the manager of this state historic site would prefer to promote the old home's rich history, too many unexplained incidents have happened to too many staff members and visitors to deny the mansion's ghostly track record.

Thus, the historical site conducts an annual "Scarefest" each October. All proceeds benefit restoration efforts at the mansion. The rest of the year the staff concentrates on conducting historic tours.

The three-story French Second Empire-style mansion was built in 1869 by one of Indiana's wealthiest businessmen, William S. Culbertson. Located in an area of New Albany now known as Mansion Row Historic District, the magnificent twenty-two room home was originally built on the site of a Civil War hospital. Several individuals feel that the hauntings are connected with this hospital, where soldiers from many horrific battles fought their own desperate battles with gangrene, dysentery and other diseases only to die in the arms of distraught relatives.

The first week that one of the curators worked at the home, he admitted to being a little nervous, especially when left alone to lock up the large and very dark house for the night. His nervousness quickly changed to apprehension and then fear when he heard footsteps, a door slamming and furniture being moved in another room. After experiencing this phenomenon on at least two other occasions, he decided to just go about his business and let "them" go about theirs.

Another curator who actually had an apartment in the mansion recalls locking the doors, turning out the lights, grabbing her two cats, dashing into the apartment and locking the door behind her. Nothing ever happened in her apartment, but ghostly happenings did take place in other parts of the house, sometimes during the day and sometimes at night. She really wasn't frightened during the day with other people around but nighttime was different. One night, while she was locking up the house, an unseen hand shoved her!

The entity seems to be fascinated by, of all things, the vacuum cleaner. On at least two occasions a staff member had finished cleaning a room, turned the vacuum cleaner off and left the room for just a few minutes when they heard the cleaner turn on. Reentering the room, staff members found dried flowers from a nearby vase scattered over the floor and the vacuum cleaner running.

There have been so many sightings by staff and visitors that a file has been created to document the events that continue to occur to this day. A family from Kentucky was recently visiting the site when the husband saw a woman wearing a long gray skirt with a bustle or bow in the back and black high-top shoes or boots walk quickly by the entrance to a second floor bedroom. She passed the doorway and then seemed to disappear into the wall.

After this sighting he went looking for the guide and his wife, who'd gone down to the first floor. These two women were in one of the parlors talking when they heard footsteps in the hall. Thinking it was the woman's husband they walked into the hallway only to find no one there. In retrospect they realized that what they'd heard were the sounds of either high heels or boots.

When people say they don't believe in haunted houses the staff smile. It's not good to disagree with paying guests.

✻ ✻ ✻

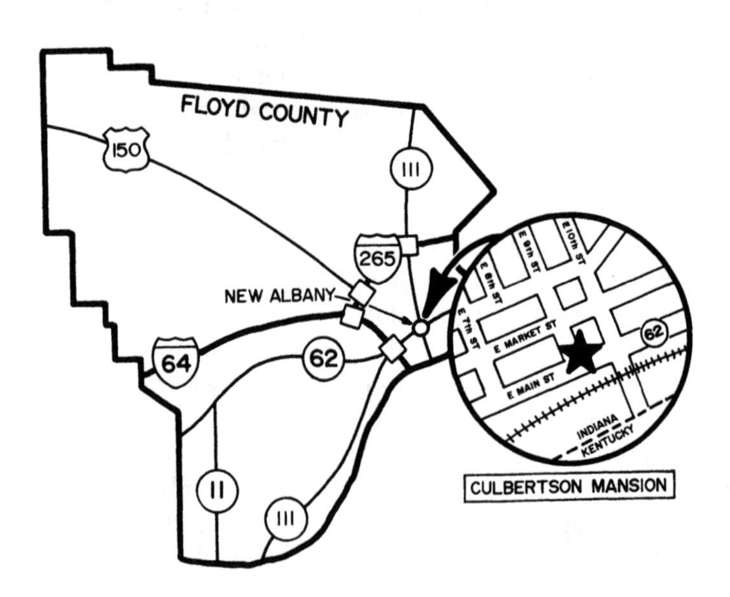

GREENE COUNTY

Greene County, named for Nathaniel Greene, a Revolutionary War general, was organized in 1821. Its hills and forested areas make it one of the most remote in the state even now, and one of the counties richest in folklore.

The county seat of Bloomfield was laid out in 1824 and named by Dr. Hallet B. Dean for his birthplace, Bloomfield, New Jersey. Bloomfield has the distinction of being the ninth smallest town in the nation to have a daily newspaper, the *Evening World.* Don Herold (1889–1966) is Bloomfield's most famous citizen. An American humorist, Harold published fifteen books, including *There Ought to Be A Law* and *Strange Bed Fellows.*

Linton, the largest community in Greene County, was settled around 1816, and was originally known as New Jerusalem.

By the 1890s the area was an important coal-mining center, but the dependency on this industry has declined since the 1940s. Many former strip mines have been converted into parks and lakes. The Linton park system is considered to be one of the best in the state. The community's livelihood is based on farming, small business, tourism and manufacturing.

Linton native Phil Harris started his career in the late 1920s as a musician and later became nationally known for his music and comedy in radio on the "Jack Benny Show," 1936–46 and the "Phil Harris/Alice Faye Show," 1946-54. Younger Hoosiers would know him for his voice-overs in Walt Disney movies.

In 1825 the town of Worthington was laid out and named for Worthington, Ohio, home of one of the founders. Situated on the Eel and White Rivers at the proposed junction of the Wabash and Erie Canal with the projected Central Canal from Indianapolis, Worthington was supposed to be destined for large-scale commercial success. The Central Canal was never completed.

The largest deciduous tree in the nation, the Big Sycamore, was located in the Worthington area. The tree stood 150 feet high, spanned 100 feet and measured at its base forty-three feet and three inches in girth.

The Legend of Poor Pollie: Linton's Beloved Eccentric

Here Pollie Barnett is at rest, from deepest grief and toilsome quest.
Her cat, her only friend, remained with her until life's end.

Pollie Barnett was born September 23, 1836, and died in Linton on February 27, 1900. Though Pollie has been gone for over a hundred years, her story still lives on in Greene County's oral tradition.

Pollie was a vagabond, roaming alone through Greene and adjacent counties, for years before her death. In her final years she was accompanied by her steadfast companion, a large black cat.

Very little is known of her life prior to her nomadic existence. The *Bloomfield Democrat* in an account of her death referred to her as, "the well known and eccentric old wanderer" of Linton. Continuing, the article stated, "There are very few people in southern Indiana who have not heard of Old Pollie Barnett. Her persistent wandering from place to place in the futile search of her long lost daughter had made her a familiar figure to the people of southern Indiana."

Why had she chosen this life, eating whatever she could find or what food kind farm women might give her? What induced her to roam the countryside enduring hardships that a man would find difficult? This is the legend which has given her a kind of immortality.

Pollie was evidently married at one time, whether divorced or widowed no one knows. What is known is that she had a daughter, Sylvanie, who disappeared under mysterious circumstances. At the time of her disappearance Sylvanie was only fifteen years old.

It's generally believed that a farmhand murdered her. The community, at least, believed he had killed the girl and buried her in a White River sandbar near Newberry. The murderer, too, disappeared.

Pollie would not accept that her daughter was dead and began a thirty-year nomadic existence, her wits addled, searching for her child. Sympathetic people in Greene and surrounding counties helped her as she passed through. Some would let her spend the night and give her and her cat a meal. Others gave her spending money, which she'd put in her shoe.

No one seemed to be afraid of her and some even let her spend a night in their homes. In 1970 a woman remembered that when she was a child, her mother kept a cot with blankets and pillow for Pollie whenever she'd come their way.

Of course, there were some that labeled her a "beggar" and a "mad woman" and kept her away from their doors. Others who remembered her from their childhoods before the turn of the century, spoke of her in interviews for the newspaper much later. They described her as a little woman with gray, scraggly hair and shabby clothes, her shoes never laced and her coat always open even in the coldest weather.

Poor Pollie never found her daughter and went to her grave not knowing Sylvanie's fate. A common theme in legends such as this is that the search continues beyond the grave, usually in ghostly form. Some believe the search does continue, but not by Pollie's ghost. On her deathbed she asked that her cat be released to continue searching for Sylvanie.

The people of Linton contributed to a burial fund and Pollie was given a Christian burial in Fair View Cemetery, on Fairview Road in Linton, and a memorial tombstone. H. H. Strietelmeier's name appears on the stone as the carver, which features the figure of a cat at rest on top of the monument. The carving is a tribute to Pollie's black cat, her loyal companion in her last years. On the side of the headstone is this inscription, "Donated by the citizens of Linton."

Perhaps with her nine lives extended into ghostly realms, Pollie's black cat wanders the hills of Greene County still.

"Here Pollie Burnett is at rest, from deepest grief and toilsome quest. Her cat, her only friend, remained with her until life's end."

Photo by Mary Witte

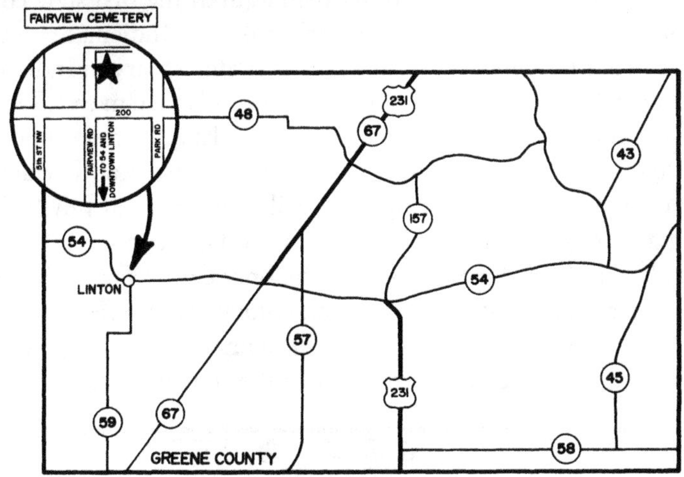

HARRISON COUNTY

Harrison County is the middle county of the thirteen Indiana counties that border the Ohio River. It is popularly referred to as the Cradle of Indiana because the state's first capital, Corydon, was located in Harrison County. The fourth county established in Indiana Territory, it was organized in 1808 and included present Washington and Floyd counties and parts of Orange, Perry and Crawford.

The county was named for William Henry Harrison (1773–1841), first governor of Indiana Territory, commander at the Battle of Tippecanoe and ninth president of the United States.

In 1804 Squire Boone settled in the area now known as Squire Boone Caverns and Village. He built the county's first gristmill at this spot. At the time of his death in 1815, the family fulfilled his request that he be buried in a small cave near the larger one.

Mauckport, platted in 1827, was named for its founder Frederick Mauck, an early settler and ferryman. In 1829 Mauckport, citing its status as a bustling river port, competed unsuccessfully with larger cities to become the southern terminus of Michigan Road. Just east of Mauckport was a place known as Morgan Landing. From this spot Brigadier General John Hunt Morgan and his raiders invaded Indiana in the summer of 1863.

The site for Corydon, the seat of government for Harrison County, had been purchased by William Henry Harrison in 1804, and was named for the shepherd in his favorite song, "Pastoral Elegy."

In June 1816, a convention called to draft the first state constitution convened in Corydon. The original 1816 Indiana State Constitution is still preserved at the Indiana State Library in Indianapolis. The delegates convened outdoors under a large elm tree. The tree would forever be known as the Constitution Elm. It stood about fifty feet high with a spread of approximately 132 feet. Another distinction came to Corydon during the Civil War when on July 9, 1863, Morgan's Raiders fought a battle with the Harrison County Home Guards near Corydon—the site of the only Civil War battle fought on Indiana soil. Today the site is commemorated as the five-acre Battle of Corydon Memorial Park. Frank O'Bannon had a law practice in Corydon before becoming governor of the state of Indiana.

The Legend of Haunted Hollow

The scenic beauty along the Ohio River, the Indian's "Beautiful River," is legendary. High limestone cliffs with small caves rim the banks. Some of the cliffs covered with ferns and mosses rise almost two hundred feet above the water, causing visitors along the river roads to gasp in admiration.

In the first decade of the 1800s, river pirates lying in wait for unsuspecting river travelers used the caves and rock overhangs on both sides of the Ohio River as their hideouts. Two miles west of Mauckport on the Indiana side was one of the pirates' favorite hiding places, a hidden location from which to leap swiftly and surely. Quite often people were killed and their possessions divided between the bandits, but always property was stolen.

A flatboat reached this ambush spot late one evening, unaware that there were pirates lurking in the area. The boatmen came ashore, lit a cozy campfire on the bank and had a pleasant dinner. Afterward all returned to the boat to sleep except for a man posted beside the smoldering fire to keep an eye out for trouble.

Making himself comfortable, the flatboat guard soon fell asleep. Suddenly he was awakened when a pirate, unaware of his presence, stumbled over him. The startled boatman jumped up and yelled out a warning. The men on the flatboat awoke, quickly cut the mooring ropes and pushed off into the river, leaving their comrade behind.

Overwhelmed by the gang of brigands, the poor man fought courageously. He was shot and stabbed repeatedly and then decapitated, with his head thrown into the river; and his body left to the wild animals.

The pirates quit harassing boatmen when settlers began moving into the area in the 1820s. But "something" remained of the terrible deed they did that night. People began reporting seeing a headless man stumbling along the riverbank.

As the stories spread, farmers, tradesmen and travelers avoided the site, which became known as Haunted Hollow. The headless ghost of the boatman was seen for many years. Even today on dark nights some local residents claim he still prowls the hollow, looking for his head.

❋❋❋

JACKSON COUNTY

Jackson County became the fourteenth territorial county when it was established in 1815. It was named to honor Andrew "Old Hickory" Jackson, who had earlier in the year stopped the British in the Battle of New Orleans. The county's boundaries became fixed in 1859, after eleven readjustments to allow for neighboring county development. It is the state's eighth-largest county. A leading melon producer, the county is agriculturally oriented, with some manufacturing concentrated in the Seymour area.

The oldest community in Jackson County is Vallonia, dating from 1810 or 1812. A version of Fort Vallonia, the principal stockade in the county during the War of 1812, has been built in the heart of the town, and each October the town holds an Old Fort Vallonia Days Festival.

Seymour is recognized as the location of the nation's first train robbery, committed by the Reno gang on October 6, 1866.

Three of the Reno brothers, Frank, William and Simeon, are buried in the Old Seymour City Cemetery. The Renos and one of their gang members (Charlie Anderson) were being held in the New Albany jail when vigilantes overtook the facility and hanged the criminals from the second level of cells on December 12, 1868. The three brothers were placed in one large pine box and buried in the cemetery three days later.

Hush Little Baby, Don't You Cry

They'd just moved into the Victorian home near the old Seymour cemetery in Seymour and everything was just about perfect. The home needed some repairs and painting, but what really mattered was that the house was theirs. Friends and family steeped in the folklore of the Midwest wondered about the location—next to that cemetery. They laughed and replied that at least their neighbors would be quiet.

About a week after they'd moved in, the wife was awakened by the sounds of a child crying. She woke her husband and asked him if he heard the child. "No," he mumbled, "You're dreaming. Go back to sleep."

From time to time she thought she heard the sound of the crying child—sometimes at night and sometimes when she was alone in the house. No one else seemed to hear what she heard. One day as she was painting the living room the child began to cry again, pitifully. She could not ignore it. The sound was coming from somewhere outside. She stepped out on the front porch and looked around to see if a child might have been playing nearby and was hurt. But there wasn't anyone else around and the crying had stopped.

The wife went back into the house and once again picked up the brush. But before she could begin to paint the crying started again, more pitifully and persistently, and as she looked towards the cemetery the crying seemed to get louder. Still no one was in sight.

The phenomenon continued off and on for several weeks. She decided to plant the flowerbeds. As she moved through the weed-ridden beds, she tripped over a rock hidden in the tall weeds behind the house.

Pulling at some of the vegetation to uncover the stone, she saw it wasn't a rock! It was a single tombstone. The name and dates were barely legible but in time she was able to determine that a child had been buried there.

When her husband came home that evening she showed him what she'd discovered. Together they began cutting and clearing around the stone thinking this had been a family plot. Amazingly they found no other stone.

The following week she went to the library searching for information pertaining to the child's parents. It was useless; no records existed as to the child's lineage. However, there were several burials with the same German surname at the Crothersville cemetery. She and her husband had the stone and the child relocated to the Crothersville cemetery. After that the crying stopped.

The Medora Haunted House

The crumbling remains of a house built in 1848 can be seen at the top of the Knobs west of Medora, Indiana, on old US 50. Its story belongs in the category of Civil War ghost tales.

Ann Wilson's youngest son, Aesop, was seventeen when he told his parents he wanted to enlist in a company of volunteers assembling at Medora in the spring of 1861. His mother forbade him to go. Although he didn't want to go against his mother's wishes, he longed to join up with his friends to save the Union. Thus, reluctantly, his parents bade him good-bye as he went to enlist in Company B, 22nd Regiment, Indiana Volunteers. He was sent to Boonville, Missouri, where his mother's worst fears were realized: her son died.

In April 1862 his father had his son's body returned to Medora for burial. However, his distraught mother would not allow her son to be buried. She insisted the undertaker place the body in charcoal and seal the casket. It was then put upstairs in his bedroom, in front of the window. For twelve years the casket remained there. Every day his mother would go upstairs and sit in a rocking chair, sew and talk to her dead son.

Her husband begged her to let him have their son buried, but she refused until in 1873, after he had hired a spiritualist from Louisville, Kentucky, to come to their house and hold a séance. During the séance they heard a voice saying, "Mother, this is your son."

The dead soldier's mother asked the voice many questions and when she was finally convinced that it was the voice of her dead child, she asked if he would like to be buried. He instructed her to have his remains buried in the cedars just north of the house and his wishes were obeyed.

Some say as they've driven by at night they have seen what looked to be a glowing white, wraith-like figure standing at the edge of a group of old cedars just north of the crumbling house. It is believed it's the ghost of the soldier on sentry watching over the family home he had left over 140 years ago. A church stands on the site today.

Trombone Tommy

A haunted railroad tunnel near Medora, between Medora and Fort Ritner, has a ghost not believed to be frightening, but rather sad.

During the 1920s and 1930s jobs were hard to find and often a man would have to travel miles from home just to earn a meager living. In many instances the unwilling vagrants were forced to become knights of the rails—hobos. Along the rails these itinerants would set up camps where all of the knights were welcome to stay, bunk under the stars and share cans of beans for as long as they wished.

One of these knights must have been a musician at one time for he always traveled with his trombone. His companions dubbed him Trombone Tommy.

People who lived in the area often talked about hearing him playing his trombone as he walked through the nearby railroad tunnel. One night, intent on playing, he evidently didn't hear a freight train enter the tunnel and was killed.

On summer evenings the town's residents had heard Trombone Tommy's music coming from the tunnel as they sat on their front porches cooling off from the hot summer's sun. Though no one in the community knew him or even had met him, they soon realized they missed him. His trombone was silent.

However, shortly after the accident, people began to hear the echoes of music coming from the direction of the tunnel. At first they were frightened, but then they accepted and enjoyed the music for what it was. Trombone Tommy was continuing to play for them even after death.

The Witch of White Chapel

Her name was Martha and she was said to be a witch. For centuries, old, eccentric women were branded as witches when their only sin was being odd. Martha is supposed to be buried in White's Chapel Cemetery on County Road 925 N southeast of Spraytown. It's said her face can be seen on the side of her tombstone.

Martha's grave is located on the edge of the cemetery, near the road and away from the other graves. Those good Christians responsible for her burial might have been afraid to place her too near their own family plots.

According to local legend, if one touches her face, the person will be in a car accident.

The manager of a local restaurant used to say that when he was a teenager, he and three others had gone out to the cemetery and as a prank pushed over the top half of Martha's tombstone. Realizing how stupid it was they decided to place it back on top of the base. The four of them together couldn't budge it.

The next day two of them returned to the scene of the desecration determined to try with all their might to set it back up. Convinced that this was probably a fruitless effort they nonetheless began to struggle with the heavy stone. Surprisingly they were able to pick up the stone by themselves and reposition it.

How could only two do what four could not? Perhaps Martha used her witch's magic to help them, deciding these two had felt so much guilt they'd even come back to correct the damage they'd help create the night before.

The mystery of her face appearing on the tombstone is the most persistent of the stories. No one has stepped forward to say they have touched the face and have actually experienced an accident.

Those daring enough to visit her gravesite claim they've seen the witch's face on the tombstone like a charcoal sketch, not always in the same place. Sometimes it flits like a shadow on the top of the stone. Not only does the face move from time to time, as if Martha is watching, it's been reported that at times it appears to be smiling and at other times frowning.

❋❋❋

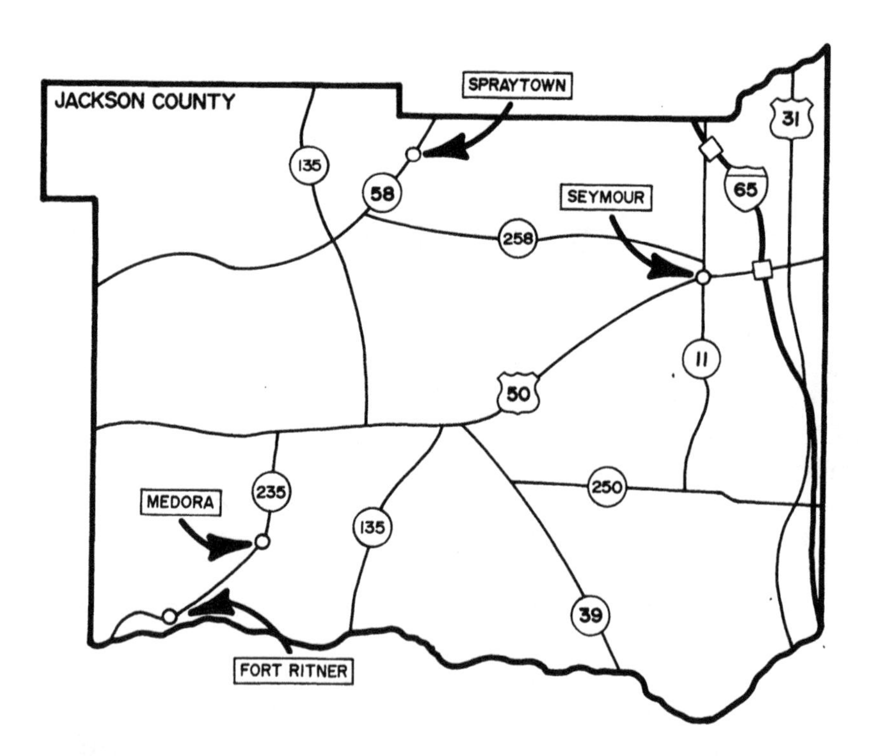

KNOX COUNTY

Knox County was the first county established in the state, and its winding roads, similar to Indian paths, attest to a different settlement time and pattern from the rest of Indiana's counties. It was named for Major General Henry Knox, a Revolutionary War artillery officer and secretary of war, 1785–1794. At its inception, Knox County extended to Canada and encompassed all or part of the present states of Indiana, Michigan, Illinois and Ohio.

The county seat, Vincennes, is the oldest continuously inhabited city in Indiana; the oldest continuously occupied home in Indiana, the George McClure home, is outside Vincennes. A French trading post possibly was established here as early as 1683 and settlers arrived before 1727, followed by the building of a fort in 1732. The fort was under command of Francois-Marie Bissot, Sieur de Vincennes, for whom the town was named about 1736 after he was captured and burned at the stake by Chickasaw Indians.

Vincennes University, recognized as the oldest comprehensive junior college in the United States, was chartered in 1806.

William Henry Harrison (1773–1841), ninth president of the United States, built his home, Grouseland, near the Wabash between 1802 and 1804. On one occasion he and Tecumseh met on the lawn of the mansion.

In a lighter vein, Red Skelton, one of the most beloved of American clowns, lived in Vincennes for his first twelve years. He and his widowed mother lived in a modest frame house until he was about twelve years old, when he left Vincennes with a traveling medicine show.

Wheatland, laid out in 1858 as Berryville, was the home of James D. "Blue Jeans" Williams who lived most of his life on a farm near Pond Creek Mills, south of Wheatland. He is buried in Walnut Grove Cemetery near the site of his old home. A thirty-foot-high monument was erected in his memory in 1883.

Dark Hollow

Nearly three hundred years ago a Frenchman, who lived upriver and just across the Wabash from Vincennes, was traveling alone to attend Holy Thursday services. He must have been a brave man for this was a time of much Indian trouble when most would not travel alone.

After being attacked by a band of Indians, he fought furiously, but was overcome, pulled from his horse and dragged into the dark hollow and decapitated. His horse, wild-eyed and mad with fear, crashed into the depths of the hollow. It is said the Indians ran in horror as the dead man's head rolled after his racing horse!

Some time later hunters found the man's horse placidly grazing by the headless body. They took the horse, but left the mutilated and decomposing corpse. For several generations the area experienced dark and furious storms on Holy Thursday nights. Those who dared to venture out reported seeing the dead man's head "rolling again," the thunder mingling with the sound of the terrified Indians howling in the night—so the story goes.

The entrance to Dark Hollow, or Robeson's Hills Hollow, as it is known today, was filled in during the construction of US Route 5 and is thus not accessible. As one crosses the Red Skelton Bridge over the Wabash there's a drainage ditch off to the right that goes down to the bottom of the ravine where the Frenchman's head is purported to roll.

Purple Head Bridge

During the bloody years of the French and Indian War, and in the early days of settlement thereafter, in what is today called Indiana, skirmishes between white settlers and Native Americans were continuously being fought along the banks of the Wabash, leaving many dead. As is the way with war, often the bodies of those fallen would not receive proper burial.

Thus it was for one Indian shaman who was killed in one of the early outbreaks of fighting. His body fell into the fast-flowing waters of the Wabash at flood time. Despite the efforts of his tribe to retrieve his body, it proved impossible. According to tribal tradition, without proper burial the soul could not go into the next realm. It would remain in torment, bound to the river through all eternity.

Today the narrow, one-lane Stangle Bridge, once used by the railroad, spans the Wabash from Vincennes to St. Francisville. According to local Vincennes lore, as one drives across the bridge, he or she can stop near the center and wait. Soon a hand will rise from the depths of the river, as if in supplication. Adventurers who stay a little longer will see the Indian shaman's bloated, luminous, purple head float up from the depths of the water with unseeing black holes where eyes once were. Silently he pleads to be returned to the land of his people and buried as befitting his status, thus releasing his soul from its watery entombment.

The Spirit of Otter Lake

In the early French days of Vincennes there lived a beautiful young girl, the daughter of a very important man in the town. He'd made arrangements for her to marry a friend of his, a man of his own age. She pleaded with her father not to make her marry this man; in doing so, she admitted that she had fallen in love with a young Frenchman.

Her father forbade her to see this young man, but young people in love will find a way to be together. When friends went to Otter Lake to fish or lazily glide in a boat her father gave his permission for her to go along. There she and her lover met. She vowed to die rather than marry the old man her father had chosen.

Her father found out about the lovers' meeting, and ordered his daughter never to leave the house again until she was wedded to the old man. The night before the wedding, as her father slept, the girl crept out of the house and to the lake. The moonlight bathed the placid waters of Otter Lake, where she'd spent warm and loving days with the man she truly cared for. With a cry of anguish the distraught young girl threw herself into the waters.

No one was surprised when they did not see her for several days. Her father said that she had not been allowed to leave the house until her wedding and that the newlyweds had moved away to live in another settlement.

One day fishermen saw the beautiful face of a young girl in the water. When they brought the body out they knew who it was. When the father saw the lifeless body of his young daughter he admitted that she'd run away the night before her wedding. He'd searched for her in vain and in desperation he made up the story of her marriage and removal to another community. Heartsick and burdened with the guilt of his daughter's death, the father took his own life.

No Frenchman trapped or fished Otter Lake for a very long time after that. Those who dared told of hearing an unearthly sound like a banshee or a wailing siren's song. They feared the girl's spirit would draw them into the lake and they, too, would drown.

Nighttime was the worst. Some said they'd hear wails across the water and see lights like two eyes traveling toward the bank; then, they'd disappear into the water and an awful, mad groan and sigh would echo across the quiet waters. The young maiden still laments her lost love.

❋❋❋

The Coal Miner's Ghosts

When the *Knox County Daily News* was located on North Main Street in Bicknell, a young man from the composing room stopped by the desk of a female reporter to chat. The ad load had been especially heavy, and he'd been required to work several nights alone. He admitted he'd heard some strange noises emanating from the two backrooms—the pressroom and the photography lab.

She was not surprised and told him not to be afraid. It was only the ghosts of coal miners. They wouldn't hurt him.

Many years earlier the two rooms had contained other businesses. The front room had been a restaurant. The other room housed the Mine Rescue Station, which stored equipment for helping to find and rescue coal miners caught in one of the all-too-frequent accidents in the southern Indiana mines.

"In the early 1940s an explosion ripped through the Panhandle mine near Bicknell, killing about a dozen coal miners," she told the young reporter. "The town's two funeral homes did not have enough space to handle all of the bodies. Some were kept in the funeral home's garages while others were brought to the Mine Rescue Station. You're not the only one to have heard spooky noises."

The young compositor couldn't believe that the woman wasn't afraid of the noises in the back room. "Oh no. My father worked with these men in the mine and he'd helped bring their bodies out. Besides, two of my uncles had lost their lives in the explosion. I feel 'protected,'" she explained. Perhaps the ghosts of the long dead miners were just returning to thank the brave men who had brought their bodies back to the surface so their families could claim them for burial.

❋❋❋

The Ghost of Sigma Pi

Vincennes' Sigma Pi fraternity headquarters, a Georgian-style mansion on Old Wheatland Road, is reported to be haunted. The ghost, so students say, may be Colonel Eugene Wharf, the original owner of the building and land. The house sits on a thirteen-acre estate once known as Rebel Hill, because it was rumored to be the meeting place for Southern sympathizers during the Civil War.

The Wharf family left the land and house to Vincennes University in the 1950s and in 1962 it was given to Sigma Pi.

The colonel's presence is manifested by roaming cold spots, lights that go on and off without the aid of a human hand, objects moving and a male voice thought to be the colonel's. No one understands what he's saying, however. The ghost has one very bad habit: turning perfectly good hot cups of coffee into undrinkable cold liquid with a gust of icy wind.

The executive director insists that the house isn't haunted. Perhaps he doesn't like coffee.

❋❋❋

The Ghostly Supervisor

In the late 1980s a newlywed couple purchased a house in Bicknell on Tunnelton Road from the estate of an elderly gentleman who'd lived in the house alone for several years after his wife had died. After his death the relatives had chosen the furniture they wanted and left the remainder, including antiques, to be sold with the house. This arrangement pleased the new owners because they wouldn't have to purchase much furniture.

There were two bedrooms, and since the new owners only needed one they decided to make the second bedroom into a dining room. The large oak kitchen table was moved into the new dining room along with a few other pieces of furniture. One evening they heard what sounded like footsteps walking around and around in that room. When they investigated, they found nothing. Thinking the noises had been their imagination, they began joking that the man who'd owned the house was checking out their decorating style.

Then they decided to make some minor structural changes. Once the work was in progress, they began hearing footsteps every night, as if the ghostly supervisor was checking on the work.

Soon he began to express his opinion of the construction that he did not seem very happy about. A hammer disappeared. After looking in all the obvious places, workers found it in the bathroom. There was absolutely no reason for anyone to have carried it into that room. Until the structural changes were completed, the couple continued to hear footsteps during the night. Tools and items needed to work with the next day would be missing and turn up in odd places. After the changes were completed, the ghostly supervisor seemed satisfied and the family no longer heard the footsteps. But the spectral presence apparently had not departed.

The wife's keys disappeared. When her husband came home, she told him about the missing keys and he agreed that the ghost would return them when he was ready. Several days went by and the keys did not reappear. Then, mysteriously one day they were found on top of the television. She thanked the ghost and promised they'd try to stay home more. After that episode the couple didn't hear the footsteps nor experience any playful antics.

A few years later they decided to do some more remodeling, this time major—adding a bedroom, a bathroom, a hobby room for the husband and a laundry room. The ghostly supervisor returned to oversee the work. Once again the couple heard footsteps as the specter checked the workmen's progress. He must have approved the plans and the workmanship, because no pranks were played. He hasn't made his presence known for quite a while.

❋❋❋

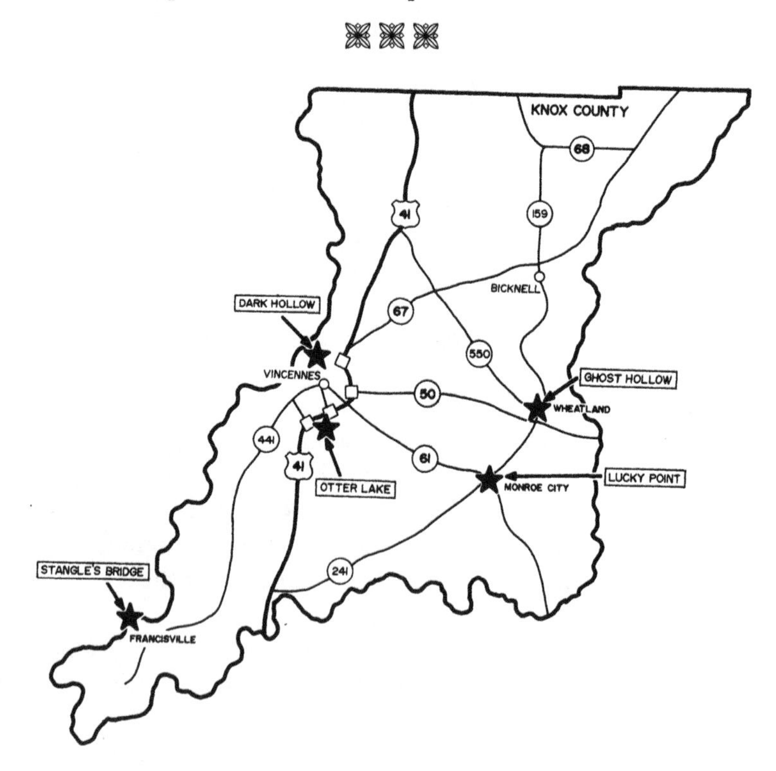

LAWRENCE COUNTY

Lawrence County was organized in 1818 and named for naval Captain James Lawrence, who died in 1813 on board his ship, the *Chesapeake*, of wounds he received during a battle with the British frigate *Shannon*. Lawrence bequeathed to the American navy a deathbed utterance that has become a rallying cry to this day—"Don't give up the ship."

Lawrence County is a part of the state's vast "Stone Belt," extending north to Putnam County and south through Owen, Monroe, Lawrence, Washington, Orange and Crawford Counties. This abundant product is known by several names: Indiana or Bedford Stone for marketing purposes, Salem for its geological formation and Oolitic for its composition.

The town of Oolitic, platted in 1888, derives its name from the geological term meaning eggstone, a reference to the resemblance of the stone's fossils to fish eggs. This is the only town in Indiana that honors a comic page hero, Joe Palooka, Champion of Democracy. The ten-foot, ten-ton stone statue stands on the lawn of the town hall and was sculpted by stonecutter George W. Hitchcock Sr. in 1948.

The county seat, Bedford, was platted in 1825 and named by Joseph Rawlins for his home, Bedford County, Tennessee. Bedford's Green Hill Cemetery has some of the finest examples of stone sculptor's craft including a girl in a straw hat, a golf bag and a doughboy.

Southwest of the town of Buddha, a crossroads church and country store hamlet established in 1895, is the site of the boyhood home of Sam Bass, the Texas train-robber.

The county is also the site of the Big Tunnel, a 1,750-foot-long railroad tunnel carved through solid rock, which is located between Tunnelton and Ft. Ritner.

The Light at the End of the Tunnel

In 1857 approximately three miles southeast of Tunnelton, the longest railroad tunnel in the state was constructed—1,750 feet long. The tunnel walls are lined with alcoves called "dead man" chambers. These are large enough for maintenance workers to find safety when a train enters the tunnel. But the name "dead man" chambers may have had even more ominous overtures. The structure has had more than its fair share of recorded deaths and unexplained happenings since it was built.

Rocks falling on the tracks from the rough-cut passage walls created a constant threat of derailments. Sometime in the late 1800s or early 1900s a watchman was walking through the tunnel with his lantern, removing rocks from the tracks. The train was early, catching the worker off guard. He had no time to reach the safety of a "dead man" chamber, was sucked under the train and decapitated. Though there's no record to substantiate this story, many people swear they have seen the man walking through the tunnel or on the hillside, carrying his lantern in one hand and his head in the other.

During World War I supplies and arms were transported through the tunnel. As a security measure against sabotage, the military posted guards at each entrance. As they patrolled the tunnel they'd pass each other midway and continue on to the opposite entrance, turn and repeat the routine. On one of these passes, one of the guards reached the middle, but the other guard did not. According to legend he was found hanging from a metal spike in the top of the tunnel. In another incident, occurring in April 1917, a National Guardsman, who was one of a two-member team guarding the tunnel, was accidentally shot and instantly killed in some sort of a scuffle with an unknown assailant. The tunnel and surrounding area was searched, to no avail. No person or evidence of anybody else having been near the tunnel was ever found.

Whether the tunnel is haunted or not, it is a dangerous place. The tunnel is still in use, and though not as many trains pass through, they are faster. If you're in the tunnel when one comes through there may not be time to seek safety in a "dead man" chamber.

❋❋❋

Chains of Destiny

The old Bond Chapel Cemetery near Huron contains many old gravesites. One of them is especially eerie. It is the grave of Floyd E. Pruett, who died in the early 1900s. Mr. Pruett, a logger, came home one evening and found his wife in bed with another man. The man got away, but unfortunately, the wife did not. Legend says her husband killed her with a logging chain, though he was never charged.

Later the husband himself was killed in a logging accident, becoming entangled in a chain. Some say his wife received her retribution from beyond the grave.

A pink granite marker etched only with his name and birth and death dates was placed on the "wronged husband" grave. However, shortly after his death visitors to the graveyard discovered the pattern of a chain in the form of a cross now appeared on the stone. The curious began visiting the site. It was discovered that the number of links forming the cross was increasing until finally there were thirteen.

Groups of teenagers began visiting the site. One night two boys decided to go on their own. One of them began counting the links, placing his finger on each one as he counted. Sure enough—there were thirteen links!

Suddenly, a light appeared among the graves; it was moving toward them. They ran back to the car and "burned rubber" getting out of the graveyard. With the eerie light pursuing them, the young driver put his foot on the gas pedal.

The road was very winding and at one of the most difficult curves the driver lost control, and the car plummeted between two guard posts connected with a chain. One of the boys was thrown from the car. Though in critical condition he did survive. But the other boy died in the crash; he'd been the one who'd touched the chain on the tombstone.

The "flawed" stone was replaced in the 1960s with another pink granite stone bearing only the man's name and birth and death dates. Shortly after it had been placed on the grave a chain in the shape of a cross began to appear on the new stone, and it, too, consisted of thirteen links.

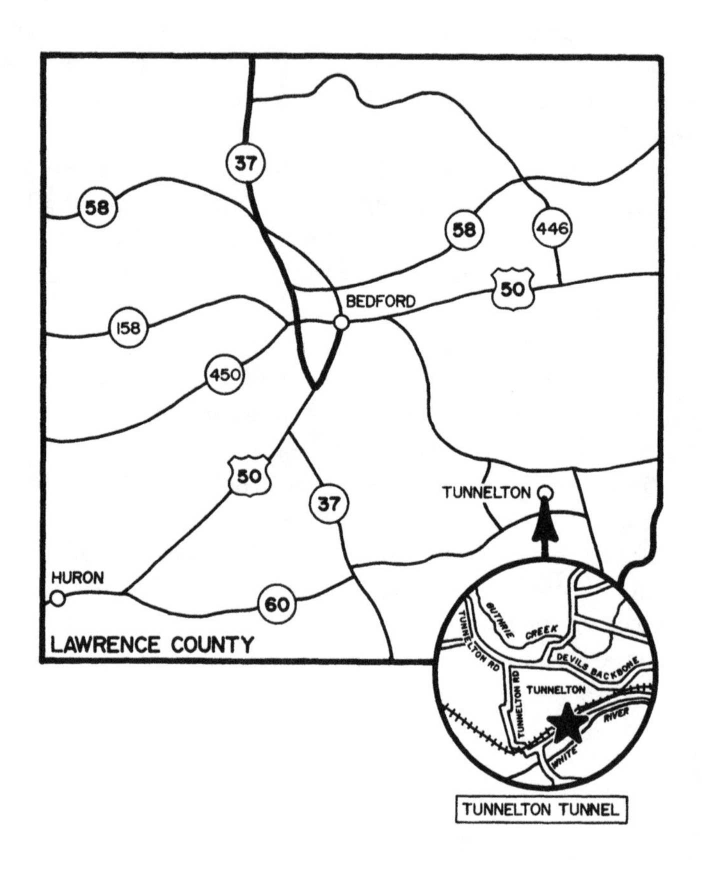
37
58
58
446
50
BEDFORD
158
450
50
37
TUNNELTON
HURON
60
LAWRENCE COUNTY
GUTHRIE
CREEK
TUNNELTON RD
DEVILS BACKBONE
TUNNELTON RD
TUNNELTON
RIVER
WHITE
TUNNELTON TUNNEL

MARTIN COUNTY

Named for Major John T. Martin of Newport, Kentucky, Martin County was formally organized February 1, 1820. Its original size consisted of only 268 square miles. Most of the land was originally from Daviess County except a portion of the southeastern part which came from Dubois County. Prior to the formation of Daviess County in 1817, much of the entire region was part of Knox County. Shoals is now the county seat, although this was not always the case. Martin County has the record for the greatest number of county seat changes. Hindostan was the first county seat. Mount Pleasant was the next county seat until May, 1844. Memphis, Harrisonville, Hillsboro (now named Dover Hill) later were designated county seats. On April 27, 1876, the court house was destroyed by fire, and pending the erection of new buildings, the offices were moved across the river to Shoals.

Martin County is located in the southwestern part of the state, about fifty miles north of the Ohio River and forty miles east of the Wabash River, or western border of the state.

In 1940 the U.S. Navy began construction of the Crane Naval Ammunition Depot. Today, the Crane Naval Weapons Center extends into Baker, Brown and McCameron Townships of Martin County and the southern edge of Greene County. In addition, Baker Township encompasses a small corner of the Hoosier National Forest.

Paoli's Bluebeard

Around Paoli they've told the tale of an old man who was the marrying type. No one remembers how many wives he had, but he certainly had a problem with them—he couldn't keep them alive. When one would die he'd marry himself another.

Sometime in the middle 1800s he had a mausoleum built in the Odd Fellows Cemetery just up School House Hill on Highway 150 on the way to Louisville, explaining that he had to have it to keep all his wives together.

He never owned a horse and wagon. He'd come down the hill into town on a little donkey, his bare feet nearly dragging the ground. He'd get a few supplies and then up the hill he and his donkey would go.

Once a week like clockwork the people would see him coming down the hill on his donkey and heading toward the cemetery. They'd been noticing a horrible odor coming from the cemetery about the time he'd go there. Finally some of the men decided to follow him. They watched as he opened the door to the mausoleum and went in. They swore that they saw him open the coffins and comb the hair of his dead wives. The odor from the coffins nearly knocked them dead.

The town made him bury his wives for sanitary and humane reasons. He finally agreed to let the undertaker take them from the mausoleum and give them a proper burial. However, two of the bodies disappeared before the burials could take place!

Everyone was suspicious of the man but no one could prove that he'd had something to do with the women's deaths. Then one day he rode his donkey down the hill and told the county judge's daughter that the sheriff better be heading up to his house. When she asked why the old man said, "My wife is goin' to be dead soon." He turned around and headed back up the hill with his bare feet dangling.

When the sheriff went to the old man's house a couple hours later the sheriff found the old man's wife dead in her bed. In another room he found the remains of what he assumed were the two missing wives that had disappeared from the mausoleum. The old man was nowhere to be found. They never did find him.

The three bodies were buried in the cemetery. Neighborhood folks used to say they could still hear that last wife hollering, yelling for help.

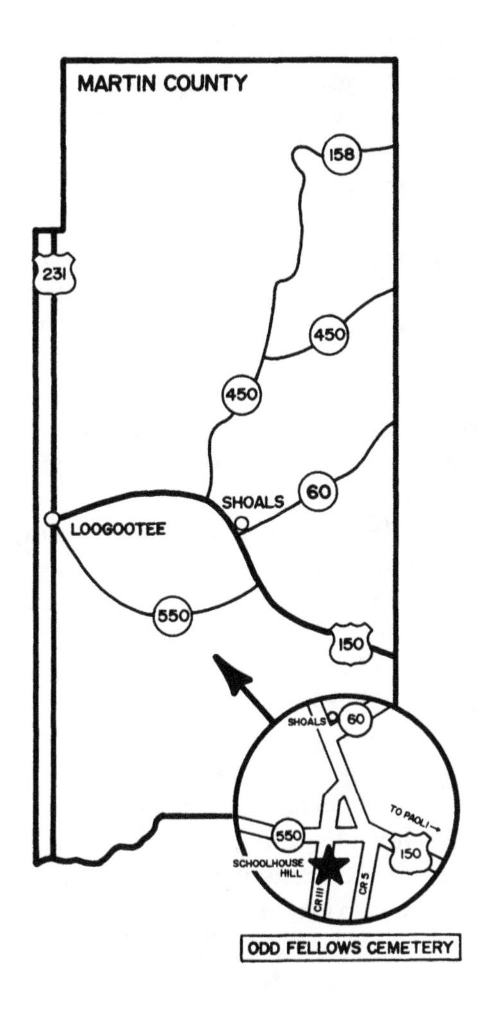
MARTIN COUNTY
158
231
450
450
SHOALS
60
LOOGOOTEE
550
150
SHOALS
60
TO PAOLI
550
150
SCHOOLHOUSE HILL
CR 111
CR 5
ODD FELLOWS CEMETERY

PERRY COUNTY

Perry County was organized in 1814 and named for Commodore Oliver Hazard Perry, who defeated the British in the Battle of Lake Erie in 1813. Half of the county is in timber, more than 56,000 acres in the Hoosier National Forest. Most of the remainder is devoted to agriculture.

Tell City, the county seat, was founded in 1857 when representatives of the Swiss Colonization Society of Cincinnati chose this Indiana river site for a new industrial city. The city was named for William Tell, the legendary Swiss hero.

As planned the city, incorporated in 1886, became a manufacturing town of mills, breweries, furniture factories and river-related industries. One of the largest employers in the community is the Tell City Chair Company, established in 1865.

In 1837 Coal Haven was founded by the American Cannel Coal Company after earlier discoveries went undeveloped. In 1847 the Cannelton Cotton Mill Company was founded and became one of the town's largest industries until its closing in 1954.

The Marquis de Lafayette, famous French general and American ally in the Revolutionary War, was supposed to have gone ashore in 1825 at Lafayette Springs after the steamboat he was traveling on struck a submerged ledge and quickly sank.

About four miles north of Rome on highway 66 is the site of Hines Raid. On June 17, 1863, Captain Thomas Henry Hines (1838—1898) took his company of sixty-two Confederate troops from Kentucky into Indiana to join John Hunt Morgan on his famous raid.

On August 21, 1865, *Argosy III*, a steamboat on its way to Cincinnati with a group of mustered-out Civil War veterans, ran into a storm near Rono. The boat was hurled against rocks and the boiler exploded, scalding some of the passengers while others jumped into the river. Ten soldiers on their way home after surviving years of the war were drowned. The veterans were buried in a mass grave, today marked by ten white stone markers.

The Ghost Rider of River Road

On September 8, 1858, the Brazee and Schuster families and friends had gathered at Mulberry Park, the Brazee's estate on River Road between Cannelton and Tell City, for the wedding of Amanda Brazee to Paul Schuster. The festivities were disrupted by the appearance of a supernatural apparition in the form of a horseman brandishing a riding crop astride a rearing horse with hoofs slashing at the air. The gathering watched as the man and beast galloped off and disappeared.

The story began circulating throughout the community and many laughed saying that the wedding party surely had been celebrating a "mite too much" and were seeing things. Chuckling, they dubbed the sighting "Brazee's ghost." Whatever it was, it had been seen by too many people for its existence to be denied.

River Road, a three-mile stretch, was once the only route between Cannelton and Tell City. For years after the first sighting of the ghost rider, many travelers reported encountering the menacing vision. On one occasion a young man, proud of his own bravery, was driving his buggy to Cannelton when suddenly the apparition made an appearance. He reined in his team, pulled out his revolver and began shooting; but his bullets had no effect. Whipping the team, he ran his buggy at full speed the final mile and a half to Cannelton. When he arrived at his home his face was as white as a sheet and the team lathered and frothing at the mouth.

About 1890 a teenage boy was hurrying along River Road from Tell City to Cannelton to reach his destination before a threatening storm. As he neared Mulberry Park a particularly loud clap of thunder shook the earth and a great bolt of lightning illuminated the road just ahead of him. There, off to the side of the road, he saw the ghost astride his rearing horse with riding crop held high. The boy turned and ran back to Tell City as fast as he could.

Today River Road is little used, an overgrown lonely stretch hidden behind the fifteen-foot floodwall erected in 1940. Brazee's once elegant home was razed long ago.

No one knows who the rider was, though there are many theories, or why he terrorized River Road for nearly fifty years. The sightings ceased after 1900, but those who encountered the ghost rider of River Road a century ago were convinced he existed.

Vengeance is Mine, Saith the Lord

When mob justice takes over, tragedy can ensue, and tragedy is the stuff of which ghost stories are made. The horror and shame of one mob violence episode has haunted Perry County for 115 years.

On May 30, 1887, a fifteen-year-old farmhand had worked all day helping his neighbor John Davidson cut wood; he spent the night at the Davidson home, located in an area known at Kitterman Corner, not far from Bristow. They did not realize that night would be the most eventful of their lives.

John's younger brother, Clay, had fallen in love with a young girl, who returned his love. The girl's father forbade her to see the young man or to even speak to him, and if Clay dared to come around he announced he'd have him beaten and she'd receive the same punishment.

One Sunday as her parents were getting ready for church the young girl told them she didn't feel well. They continued on to church leaving her home alone. As soon as they were out of sight she ran to the woods where her lover waited. They ran away determined to marry. When her parents came home and found her gone, they suspected what had happened.

The father rode from one friend's home to the other telling them what he knew to be a lie, that Clay Davidson had kidnapped his daughter and no telling what he would do to that poor, innocent, chaste girl.

Night fell; men saddled their horses, blackened and donned their white hoods. The earth trembled with the sound of pounding hooves as the "White Caps," an independent social vigilante group that dominated much of the area, rode to the Davidson farm.

Sometime during the night the household was awakened by the sound of a large group of horsemen riding into the yard. Before they could react, masked men rushed into the room where the boy farmhand and John Davidson were sleeping. The men pulled them from the bed and dragged them outside.

They began hitting the two, asking repeatedly where they could find Clay Davidson. When the vigilantes were told by the boys over and over again that they didn't know where Clay was, the two were tied together and dragged through the woods, all the while being hit, kicked and pounded with sticks and gun butts. The young farmhand tried frantically to get his knife out of his pocket. Finally succeeding he was able to cut through the ropes that bound him to the Davidson boy and made a dash for safety.

The men let him go—they were intent on making Clay's brother tell them where Clay was hiding. John pleaded with them to free him or at least let him have one free hand so he could defend himself.

The vigilantes finally stopped at an oak tree and one of them, playing with a length of rope on his saddle, said, "Well, maybe this will improve your memory. Of course, it's just a suggestion."

John Davidson still replied that he didn't know where Clay was.

The inevitable happened—the angry mob hung John that night, his body left swinging while the vigilantes went back to their farms to sleep.

About two weeks later the couple returned to Perry County. No one seemed to care that they'd married. The young girl was pulled from the arms of her husband and locked in her room at her father's home. Clay was put under arrest for kidnapping and rape. Tried and convicted he was sent to prison, where he caught tuberculosis and was paroled to go home and die.

Everyone heard the "true" story that Clay Davidson and the girl had planned to elope and be married—she had willingly gone with him into Kentucky where they'd been married.

The black-faced white cappers who'd hung John Davidson stayed low and felt that they were safe. No one could identify them. They forgot about the young boy who'd gotten away that night, who had made his way into Kentucky and stayed with relatives for a time. His relatives convinced him he had to go back and accuse those men, bring them to trial.

Though he hadn't seen their faces he had recognized the voices of some of the more prominent farmers of the area. When the sheriff went out to arrest them they implicated others until by the time the trial started the court brought action—or tried to—against many of the community's citizens. Each admitted he'd been in the "posse," but maintained that he hadn't lynched John and hadn't seen who did. The young boy's testimony identifying individuals by their voices was not enough to convict any one man for murder. They all went free.

John Davidson was buried in the Fox Ridge Cemetery, a fieldstone marking his gravesite. Today, if you look hard enough, you will find a dark gray tombstone, almost black in color, with a hangman's noose deeply engraved and the inscription, "Vengeance is mine, saith the Lord."

What's Going on at the Tell City Library?

The Tell City Public Library, at the corner of 9th and Franklin, was opened to the public in 1917; since then it has been remodeled twice, doubling its size and adding a public meeting room.

One night, Debbie Seibert worked late in an effort to update some information on the server. Intent on her work, Debbie was startled when the intercom buzzed. Since the library was closed she thought another employee might have come in and buzzed from the kitchen area downstairs. She went down to the kitchen and found no one. She went back upstairs and again, the intercom buzzed and once more she found no one downstairs.

When she went back upstairs the second time, she discovered the hall light had been turned off and on the floor was a small black book about the Civil War in Perry County.

When she told Assistant Director Paul Sanders about the strange occurrences she'd experienced, he smiled slightly and nodded. He had had his own strange occurrences.

He, too, had stayed late one night after all patrons had left. He went out the front door, turned to lock it, and saw someone going up the stairs to the second floor. Cautiously he began ascending, all the while calling out. He executed a fruitless, nervous search of the rooms on the second floor.

Once Debbie and Paul began talking about these experiences they learned that both Bookmobile Director Kay Seibert and her assistant, Brandi Sanders, whose offices are on the first floor, have heard strange sounds coming from the floor above them when they've been alone in the building.

All of the employees have heard books falling on the floor. When they've investigated they find nothing amiss. No longer will any of the employees stay alone at the library after hours.

Recently, Debbie went to the basement looking for some books in the storage area, when three books, several bookshelves away from where she was standing, came off the shelf and landed on the floor. No one had been near them and nothing could have jarred them from their shelf.

At this printing the library collection is scheduled to be moved into a new building. Will the mysterious force move with the books or stay in the old library? Only time will tell.

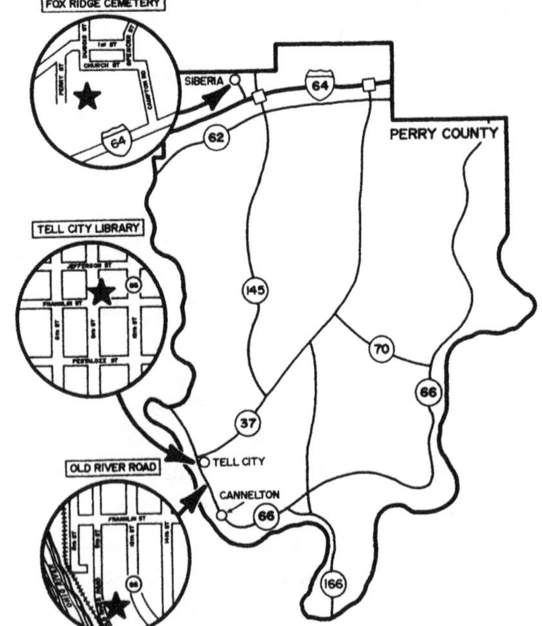

PIKE COUNTY

Pike was the first county established after Indiana statehood. It was named for Brigadier General Zebulon Montgomery Pike, a veteran of the War of 1812 and discoverer of Colorado's Pike's Peak.

The early settlers created a community around the White Oak Springs Fort, built by Woolsey Pride, along the old Buffalo Trace between Clarksville and Vincennes for protection of early settlers.

According to county tradition the last bear was shot in 1850 along Prides Creek; in this year the Wabash and Erie Canal came to Pike County. During this period, wildcats and cougars frequently assaulted inhabitants, canal workers and travelers, especially in the vicinity of Velpen.

Petersburg became the county seat in 1817. Gil Hodges (1924–1972) of baseball fame, who played for both the Brooklyn and Los Angeles Dodgers and later managed the Washington Senators and the New York Mets is a prominent native. The bridge across the East Fork of White River was named for Hodges.

A high concentration of bituminous coal deposits was discovered in 1860. At that time strip mining operations began with the Kindill #1 mine near Coe, which has been in continuous operation since that date, making it the oldest operating mine in the United States. Coal mining and the two power generating plants—the Hoosier Energy REC, Inc. and Indianapolis Power and Light Company, located on the White River just north of Petersburg, are the county's major businesses.

The coal industries reclamation programs have provided additional natural settings for the county, increasing the number of whitetail deer, otter, wild turkey and other game animals and recreational areas. The county covers 338 square acres, with 7,000 acres of waters and twenty miles of wetlands, a state forest, wildlife area and county park, all offering access to natural beauty.

Dead Man's Prophecy

Many ghost folktales involve death predictions.

A nineteenth century man who had a farm just south of Petersburg was washing up after a hard day's work, when he turned to his wife and predicted the date of his death. He warned her not to let the undertaker embalm him or bury him! If they did all the trees on the farm would die and the well and pond would dry up.

What nonsense, his wife must have thought. On his insistence she promised that his body would not be embalmed or buried. The farmer continued to work his farm in apparent good health. Summer "came on fierce" that year—hotter than Hades, some said.

During one of those hot summer days the farmer keeled over dead on the exact date he had prophesied. The local undertaker was prepared to perform the embalming when the farmer's wife intervened, telling him that she'd promised her husband that he would not be embalm nor buried. The undertaker agreed not to embalm the farmer, but insisted he would have to be buried.

At the time of the farmer's death it was customary to have a three-day wake. The deceased would be dressed in his or her finest and laid out at home until the burial. Friends and family would take turns sitting-up with the body during this period.

Because of the extremely hot summer, this farmer's wake was for one day and night only. The next day he was buried.

His wife had not completely fulfilled her promise to her husband. He was not embalmed. But she did not fulfill his wish not to be buried. The following year the rest of his prophecy came true. The trees on the farm died and the pond and well went bone dry. His widow eventually had to sell the farm and move in with her daughter's family.

By this time everyone in the area had heard about the farmer's prophecy. People claimed they'd seen the farmer walking the dead woods and heard him moaning.

Perhaps he believed he would "return," and could not.

The sons and daughters of those who knew the farmer and his wife are still telling this story in Pike County.

❋❋❋

Flat Creek Terror

The terror began for Herman Loesier on March 1, 1883. He had a good farm and sturdy house near Flat Creek just outside of Otwell.

It had been a long cold winter. Loesier was looking forward to getting his crops in in the spring. Sitting by the fire, rocking and smoking his pipe he felt pretty contented. But soon that would end.

He jumped, his heart pounding, startled by the sound of a shrill screech just outside his window, then, silence. Though shaken, he scolded himself for being afraid of a screech owl. It couldn't have been anything else. He then retired.

Herman was a bachelor and did for himself. The next morning he went into the kitchen to fix breakfast and found sugar, flour and coffee spilled on the cabinet and the floor. Scratching his head he began cleaning up the mess, thinking that some critter got in somehow.

The rest of the day was normal. He finished up his chores and drove into Otwell for some supplies, returning as darkness just began to close in. Turning down his lane he noticed what looked like a dim light in his window. This was very odd. Cautiously he opened the front door and entered the house. Stunned, he stood frozen in the doorway. "What in tarnation!" he cried.

Tables, chairs, all the furniture was overturned and tossed about as if someone or something had gone into a rage. He grabbed the shotgun he kept propped against the kitchen wall just off the front room and checked inside the house, barn and chicken coop—nothing, no one was to be found.

He went to his neighbors the next day to ask them if they'd seen any ragtags in the area lately and told them about the strange things that'd been happening over at his place. They hadn't seen any strangers.

The next few days were worse. Herman would hear the screeching sound outside his window; he'd grab his shotgun determined to give the intruding force what it deserved. Trying to scare a decent person half out of his wits! Whoever—whatever it was—got away.

He decided to go to bed. Just as he started to fall asleep he heard what sounded like an explosion and the house shook. Jumping from his bed he looked around in confusion. Nothing was wrong. Maybe he'd had a dream. Getting back into bed he tried to put the sound out of his mind when the moaning started, faintly at first as if in the distance and then louder and louder until it broke into a shriek!

Herman didn't mind telling his neighbors he was "plumb scared" out of his wits. The farmer was just about ready to admit all of this must be his imagination or nightmares when on the night of March 21, 1883 the noises started up again— screeching, insane laughter, pounding at the doors, tapping at the windows and loud explosive sounds. He cowered in a corner of his bedroom until daylight.

He didn't dare go to his neighbors again, they'd surely think he was a mad man. Though tired and shaken, he was managing to get through the day but he dreaded the nighttime. The terror at Herman's place, however, wasn't waiting for night. After finishing some chores, he was crossing from the barn to the house when he heard hysterical laughter, shrieks, loud moaning, pounding and banging all coming from inside the house. He ran to the barn and waited. It kept getting louder; he determined to return to his house. As he neared the house the sound came at him, rushing from the house with such intensity he felt as if he'd been hit with a large rock. He staggered backward into the barn determined the next day he was getting out of there—for good.

The following morning, March 23, 1883, Herman Loesier gathered his belongings and left for Otwell. The mysterious noisy monster had won.

The noises coming from the house became so loud and strange that the neighbors in the area were frightened. No one dared to go near the house, which most certainly was possessed, they claimed.

The house no longer exists. Where exactly it once stood no one knows, but even a screech owl sounding off in the vicinity is enough to make a local resident shudder.

❋❋❋

The Gullick House Ghost

By 1941 Petersburg's beautiful three-storied Gullick house had stood for more than eighty years at the corner of 9th and Main Streets. It was to be razed to make way for a gas station. By all reports this had been an impressive city landmark, built between 1848 and 1860 by Jackson M. Kinman, a successful local merchant.

The walls of the brick house were eighteen inches thick. The six-pane windows in the "magnificently proportioned house" were reported to be twelve feet long and four feet wide. Ceilings rose fourteen feet above yellow poplar floors.

The first two floors were each divided into four spacious rooms, each having a fireplace with marble mantel. In the custom of the time, the third floor was not partitioned and could be used as a playroom, ballroom, and storage.

The Kinman family enjoyed their beautiful house for only a short time before the Civil War struck, and several young men from Pike County enlisted. Richard, the only son, became Pike County's first casualty.

His body was returned to Petersburg and his family's home, where he lay in state in the west drawing room for three days. The funeral was held on the third day. His mother refused to allow him to be buried, and ordered the coffin taken to the attic where for days she'd sit and mourn the loss of her firstborn, her only son.

Finally, she was convinced to let him be buried. Soon afterward Mr. Kinman sold the house to Reuben Case and his father-in-law, James Graham, both successful stockmen. The Case-Graham family, along with the Case's two little girls, Sarah and Hattie, moved into the house.

The little girls were thrilled with the knowledge that the third floor was their playroom, until one day they climbed the stairs and entered the attic and saw in one of the shadowy corners a figure of a young man in uniform.

Running quickly out of the room they told their parents that someone was in the attic. The Cases assured them no one was there. But, upon the little girl's insistence, they investigated; finding nothing, they reassured the girls that what they had seen was only a shadow, or their imagination.

After that day the girls would enter the attic with bated breath and frightened glances over their young shoulders, toward the shadowy corner, fearing the sight of the soldier boy.

Neighbors told the parents the story of the grieving Kinman mother keeping her son's body in the attic until she was convinced by the husband to allow his burial.

After a while the little girls became used to seeing the military specter and would even share little girl secrets with him; though he never spoke, he would watch them play and then "leave."

Several years later, as young women, from time to time they seemed to be drawn to the attic for various reasons and there they would see him again. Soon they realized that there was a pattern to these appearances. Usually they occurred on the same date and month. Could this have been the date of his death?

The young Hattie married and became Mrs. Gullick and the newlyweds moved into the family home. Eventually only Hattie was left. With her grown children and grandchildren by her side the elderly woman sadly watched while the once grand home was torn down in 1941.

Later she told her family about the soldier boy in the attic and wondered what had happened to him with no attic to haunt.

❋❋❋

SCOTT COUNTY

Scott County is Indiana's fifth-smallest county. Created from parts of five existing counties in 1820, it is named after the Revolutionary War veteran and Kentucky governor Major General Charles Scott.

Centerville became the county seat. On the court house lawn is a bronze eighteen-foot tall statue of Scott County native William Hayden English (1822–1896), who was born in Lexington. English's many achievements included four terms in Congress (1853–1861), the Democratic Party nomination for vice president in 1880, the building of the English Opera House and Hotel in Indianapolis, and the writing of a history of George Rogers Clark's Revolutionary War campaigns in the Northwest Territory.

Approximately 4.7 miles south of the court house on US 31 is a marker indicating the location of the Pigeon Roost State Historic Site, where two dozen or more pioneers were killed in a skirmish with Indians over hunting rights and issues of the War of 1812.

As the timber gave out in the wooded countryside near Austin, a canning industry grew with the founding of the Austin Canning Company in 1899 by Joseph F. Morgan and others. The Morgan Packing Company today is a major food packer. The American National Can Company came to Austin in 1933 to produce containers primarily for the Morgan cannery.

Just one and a half miles from Austin at the Marshfield Station of the Jeffersonville, Madison and Indianapolis Railroad in the spring of 1868, the notorious Reno gang pulled off one of the most lucrative train robberies in American history. The Marshfield caper netted the Renos and their henchmen over $96,000 and earned them instant nationwide fame.

Poor Mary

In the 1890s the county built a three-story brick building at 1050 S. Main in Scottsburg to house its indigents and mentally ill citizens; it served the county as a "poor farm" until 1960. After that, the space was used for various county services.

Today it's being renovated for use as the Scott County Historical Society.

When the building was turned into office space there were still three elderly inmates living there. They were relocated in one of the county's retirement facilities. This left the building empty—or, at least, so it seemed.

Jeannie Carlisle's office was in the building for nearly twelve years during the time she worked for Scott County's Purdue Cooperative Extension Service. During this period she and other workers began hearing and seeing strange events.

Often she would arrive at the office before the other workers. During one of these early morning periods, she heard the front door open, then heavy footsteps like a man wearing heavy work shoes. The steps continued to a foot or two from the stairway and then stopped.

When she mentioned her observation to one of her co-workers more familiar with the poor farm and home, she was told the details and history of the place. It raised more questions than it answered, but still work had to go on.

Since there was more than one exterior door, public access bells were installed to alert the employees that someone wished to come in. Soon afterward employees who'd arrive early or stay late began reporting that the bells would ring with no one seemingly ringing them.

One Sunday morning a worker went to the building to get something from her second floor office. As she was unlocking her door, she heard a woman call her name; the employee found no one else in the office. Two students later had also heard their names called and felt a woman's presence.

The employees began calling the "visitor" Mary, after a woman with a mental problem who had lived out her life in the building when it had been the poor farm. Mary, it was said, disturbed the rest of the residents by calling out to them and talking constantly. Some say there's some mystery surrounding Mary's death. She presumably was found in bed strangled!

The grandchildren of the caretakers for the home in the late 1940s to the 1950s used to visit with their parents, but today they say you couldn't pay them enough to spend the night in the building. As children they were frightened when they had to spend a night there with their parents and grandparents because there were too many noises: the sound of doors opening and closing, someone walking in the halls and a woman constantly talking.

No one doubts that the building has experienced many sad events in its lifetime, and one may have involved poor Mary, who cannot rest even at this late date.

❋❋❋

Day is Done, Gone the Sun

Many folktales are generational, passing from grandmother to father or mother to children.

One southern Indiana family has such a story. According to their family tradition in the late 1800s, the great-grandfather had purchased a small Scott County farm. The old homestead southwest of Austin near the Washington and Scott county line had been abandoned and neglected for several years. The barn and other outbuildings needed some work, but the house was in fairly good shape, though dusty and littered with the debris of several past seasons and rodents. It needed a few panes of glass, roof repairs and a good scrubbing.

The house was ready and the farmer's relative moved in before the arrival of winter. The following year he planted his fields and mended the barn and other buildings.

Sitting on the front porch one hot July evening, he heard a knocking sound coming from the front room. Each evening about the same time the knocking resumed. This was a mystery that needed solving. He refused the idea that his house was haunted. He didn't believe in ghosts. Finally he determined that the sound was coming from within the wall between the stairs and the room.

With a crowbar he began removing the boards. To his astonishment and horror he found two skeletons dressed in Confederate uniforms. The family story states that there was no identification with them. The great-grandfather paid to have them properly buried.

Could they have been a part of the daring raid into southern Indiana in July 1863 led by the "thunderbolt of the Confederacy," General John Hunt Morgan? Had a southern sympathizer secreted them there for protection? Or had they been shot while trying to steal horses and been incarcerated there? There were many battlefields and many men missing in action. This farm may have been the sight of a small scrimmage. These two men could have fallen to their deaths—without a proper burial. Taps never sounded for these sons of Dixie.

❋❋❋

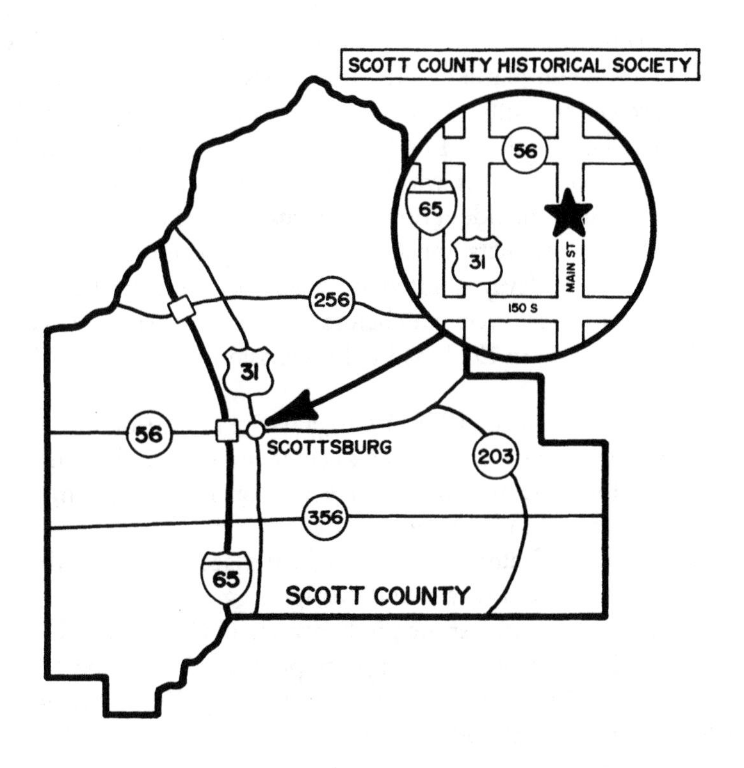
SCOTT COUNTY HISTORICAL SOCIETY
56
65
31
MAIN ST
150 S
256
31
56
SCOTTSBURG
203
356
65
SCOTT COUNTY

SWITZERLAND COUNTY

The picturesque rolling countryside and rural charm of Switzerland County remain unspoiled primarily because no railroads or giant industries exist within its boundaries.

The county seat of Vevay, originally called New Switzerland, was settled in 1802 and platted in 1813 by Swiss immigrants. The early settlers terraced the hills, planted grapes and produced wine, leading to the area's being called "The Vineyard." Besides wine the settlers also made various brandies, whiskies and beers. Eventually the town's economy became dependent on raising cattle and sheep and the production of dairy products, tobacco, hay and soybean crops.

The town of Vevay is noted for its exceptional collection of old homes, many of which were built before 1883. This concentration drew Hollywood to Vevay in 1974 to film the television movie, *A Girl Named Sooner.*

Dr. Elwood Mead (1858–1936), a native of Patriot, located on a deep channel of the Ohio, served as chief engineer in the construction of the Hoover Dam, and the huge lake formed by the dam, Lake Meade, was named in his honor.

Switzerland County was also the birthplace of nineteenth century Hoosier authors Edward and George Eggleston.

One of the wealthiest men in Switzerland County was Ulysses P. Schenck (1811–1884), a farming entrepreneur who transported hay on his fleet of Ohio River boats. Both of the magnificent Greek Revival-style homes that had belonged to the Hay King and his son, Benjamin Schenck, are today privately owned elegant bed and breakfast facilities.

In the town of Lamb can be found what is believed to be the state's oldest extant brick house, built between 1798 and 1803 by George Ash, an early pioneer and possible pirate.

A Gentle Presence

Benjamin Franklin Schenck, son of a wealthy farmer and owner of the *Vevay Weekly News*, built his thirty-five-room mansion in 1874. The impressive house, located at 206 W. Turnpike Street, with its four-storied tower, four porches, seven balconies, eight chimneys and numerous windows, was and is an architectural marvel. Schenck died just two years after moving into his newly finished mansion.

Through the years the mansion has changed hands several times. In 1999 Mr. and Mrs. Jerry Fisher purchased the home and with loving care brought it back to its original grandeur. It is now a premier bed and breakfast facility.

When the Fishers purchased the Schenck mansion, they were aware that they'd acquired something extraordinary. However, they had no idea how unusual it was.

The house was not just representative of an 1870s Norman Revival castle; it came complete with a gentle presence from the past that has been felt or experienced by some of the Fishers' guests. This was not surprising to many of Vevay citizens who have heard the tragic story of two young lovers who once lived on the site before the mansion was built.

Approximately ten to fifteen years prior to the construction of the Schenck mansion the site had contained the small house of a young girl and her lover, a Civil War soldier. Some of the citizens were very concerned with this situation—living together without benefit of clergy was not proper in Victorian society.

One night the house caught fire. By the time a fire brigade could be formed and rushed to the scene the house was completely engulfed in flame. There was nothing that could be done for the couple trapped in the house. As the brigade fought to keep the flames from spreading, people began speculating as to the origin of the fire. A few watching the horrible destruction may have likened it to the flames of Hell consuming the sinners. Others wept and wondered: was it an accident?

Is the presence guests experience the young girl who died with her lover in that fire so long ago?

Oddly, women don't see the girl; only men report seeing a young girl out of the corner of their eyes. When they turn to look, the apparition is gone. Sometimes she's seen walking into a room; the room is then found to be empty.

Lisa Fisher, one of the owners, has been told by some of her male guests that they've actually felt a gentle kiss on the cheek when they've been alone.

Though the women haven't seen anything or had any contact, they do report feeling that they are not alone.

Mrs. Fisher has photographed every room in the house except the tower room. She can't explain it, but every time she attempts to take the picture her camera refuses to work, or if it does, the film does not develop.

A friend of the Fishers was visiting one evening when a loud crashing sound came from upstairs. Mrs. Fisher was undisturbed by the sound, explaining it was the "other" guest. The Fisher family has become familiar with the various activities attributed to the presence they share the house with.

❋❋❋

The Music of the Night

A Switzerland County legend records the sad tale of a pretty young girl, the daughter of an aristocratic émigré from Europe who brought his family to the county when it was still no more than an untamed wilderness. He'd left his home, dragging his family with him to find the American Dream.

His pretty daughter, an accomplished pianist, begged him to let her stay behind with other family members so that she could continue her music lessons. He promised as soon as they were settled in America, he would get her another piano. Her anguish was so intense he suspected there was another reason for her not wanting to leave. When she admitted she was in love with her piano teacher, her father still insisted she go with the family to America.

Arriving in Switzerland County, instead of a dream they found a nightmare. It was an rough land filled with wild animals, disease and Indians. They were unprepared for the hardships of the Indiana frontier.

With help from other émigrés the father built a substantial log home with a loft near what would become Vevay. The father prospered and kept his promise to his daughter in the hope that purchasing a spinet would bring her happiness. Instead she became even sadder; the music reminded her of the love she'd left behind. She refused to play the piano.

The sturdy log home remained long after the family had died or departed. Many spoke of looking through the windows and seeing the heartbroken daughter's old, dusty, cobweb-covered spinet still in the house. Those who lived nearby believed the house was haunted, telling of often hearing the old piano playing in the night.

A few brave souls crept up to the house and watched in amazement as a beautiful young girl, who, dressed in silks and laces, would descend from the loft, and arranging herself at the little spinet and began to play her ghostly music of the night.

The date of their arrival, their names, the location of the log home and what happened to the family has not been preserved. Only in the dusty annals of Switzerland County folklore can the pretty girl's sad story be found.

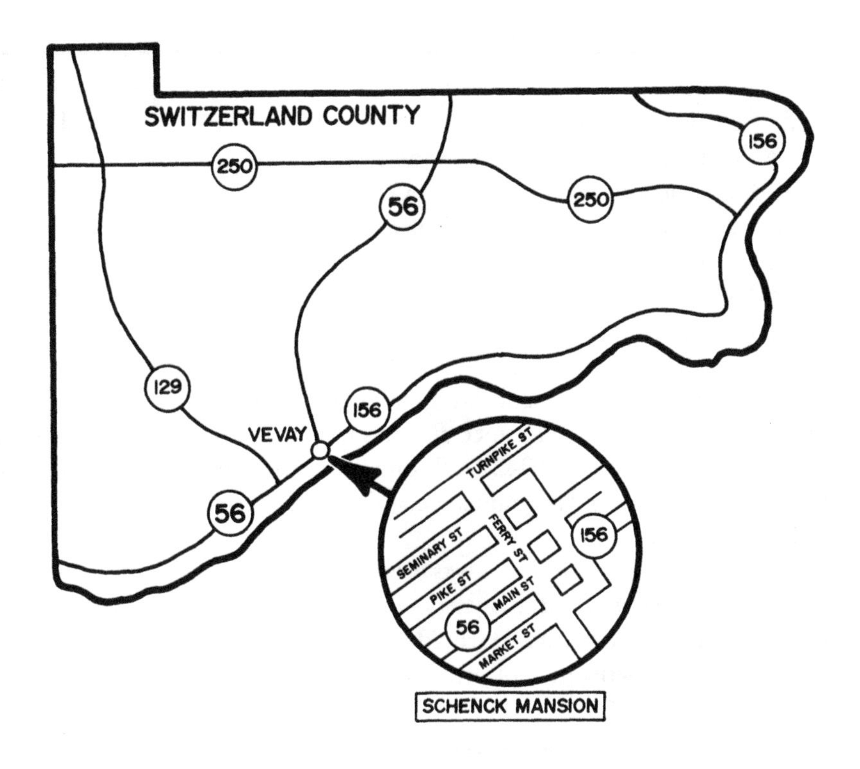
SWITZERLAND COUNTY
250
56
250
156
129
156
VEVAY
56
TURNPIKE ST
SEMINARY ST
FERRY ST
PIKE ST
MAIN ST
MARKET ST
156
56
SCHENCK MANSION

WARRICK COUNTY

Warrick County, organized in 1813, was named for Captain Jacob Warrick, who was killed in the Battle of Tippecanoe.

Boonville was selected as the county seat in 1818. It was slow to grow until 1873 when the arrival of the Lake Erie, Evansville and Southwestern Railway stimulated building and production in the coal and tobacco trades. Soon Boonville eclipsed Newburg as the most populous community and remains the county's largest city with coal mining and related industries still employing the bulk of its residents.

A feature of the present day court house is its lofty town-clock tower. The court house entrance also has a marker-commemorating William Fortune (1863–1942), a Boonville native and early editor of the *Indianapolis News* who gained recognition for his many civic works in Indianapolis.

The village of Folsomville was originally called Lickskillet. Folklore tradition states that the settlers of this village were so poor they had no utensils to eat with and would "lick the skillet clean." The town was renamed for Benjamin Folsom who had laid out the village in 1859.

The Ditney Man

On March 2, 1827, Congress provided a land grant to encourage Indiana to build the Wabash and Erie Canal through the state forming the longest canal in the United States. A section of this canal was to be built in Warrick County.

Sturdy, Irish laborers built the canals. It was punishing work, with disease and lawlessness the worst scourges. Many workers fell ill and died from ague and malaria or from injuries or barroom fights. In the mid-1800s a smallpox epidemic hit one of the canal camps, located near the town of Millersburg.

Several of the Irishmen died during this epidemic. The foreman ordered the able-bodied workers to dig a pit to be used as a mass grave. He further ordered them to gather the seriously ill who probably would die in any event and bury them along with the dead.

As if this wasn't horrible enough, some of the workers told of one of those seriously ill men awakening from a feverish sleep to find himself in the bottom of the grave surrounded by the dead. He pushed his way through the mass of corpses until he could begin to dig and claw his way to the surface, all the while vowing revenge on the foreman. By the time he reached the surface, he was quite mad. Weakened by his illness and ordeal he regained his strength by eating the putrefying flesh of those buried with him.

One night piercing screams awakened the surviving workers in their tents. Afraid to investigate, they huddled together throughout the night waiting for daylight. The next morning they cautiously crept about the campsite and discovered the foreman's body lying in a pool of blood, his chest ripped open, his heart missing.

At first it was believed that he'd been attacked by a wild animal until a few days later they discovered that someone in the burial pit had been alive and dug his way out. That the butchery was the work of this Irishman was never doubted.

As the years passed, until the last quarter of the nineteenth century, people living around the Millersburg area reported on moonlit nights seeing the specter of a man, roaming the fields along the path of the old canal. He was described as being a tall wild man, with long hair and a beard, and he waved his long fingernails menacingly like sharp knives.

Farmers occasionally reported they'd find livestock in the fields with their hearts ripped out. They never doubted this was the work of the crazed Irishman's ghost.

Because his Christian name was not known, and because he was seen most frequently near the highest point in the area—Ditney Hill—he became known as the Ditney Man.

❋❋❋

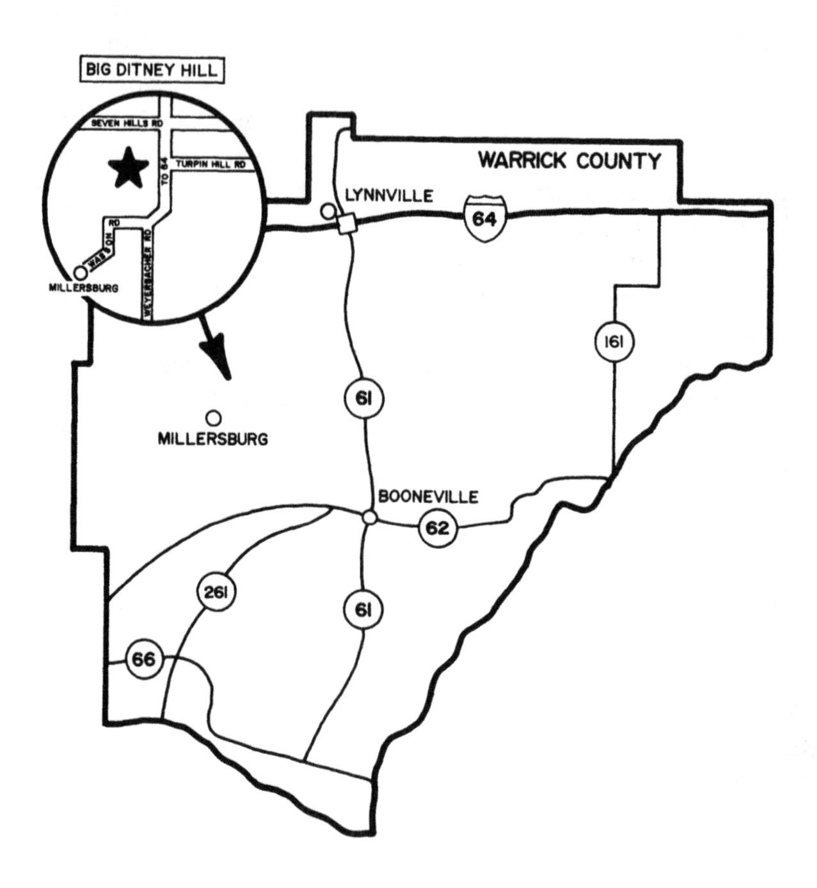
BIG DITNEY HILL
SEVEN HILLS RD
TURPIN HILL RD
TO 64
WASSON RD
WEYERBACHER RD
MILLERSBURG
WARRICK COUNTY
LYNNVILLE
64
161
61
MILLERSBURG
BOONEVILLE
62
261
61
66

WASHINGTON COUNTY

Washington County was formed from Harrison and Clark Counties in 1813 and named for George Washington.

Salem, the county seat of Washington County, was platted in 1814 and named for Salem, North Carolina. Overcoming squirrel invasions, cholera epidemics, Morgan's raiders, floods and tornadoes, Salem continued to survive and serve the region as a small agricultural and manufacturing center.

On the south lawn of the court house is a marker telling the story of Confederate Brigadier General John Hunt Morgan's stop in Salem on his raid through Indiana, cutting telegraph wires, stealing horses and property, and appropriating dinners before he was caught in Ohio.

Salem citizen Lee Sinclair (1836–1916), operator of a woolen mill and dry goods business and after 1879 the president of the State Bank, is noted for the construction of the magnificent West Baden Springs Hotel.

Another famous citizen of Salem was Christopher Harrison (1775–1863), who became Indiana's first lieutenant governor in 1816 and resigned in 1818 in a power dispute with first governor Jonathan Jennings.

The Pekin Ghost

In 1977 Robert and Pam French purchased the 1863 farmhouse located at 8178 S. State Road 335 in Pekin, Indiana. The first Halloween they lived in the house they decorated with jack-o-lanterns and purchased candy in anticipation of trick-or-treaters. None came, though they could see children going to houses near them. When they mentioned this to some of their neighbors, they were told the children were afraid to go to their house because it was haunted.

The Frenches had been in the house for about a year when Pam was dusting and realized that when she turned her back, small items such as pictures or figurines would mysteriously be moved from one spot to another.

The following year Pam finally saw the ghost, a slim, barefooted young boy, about seven or eight years old. His dark hair was cut in the bowl style and he wore bib overhauls and a shirt. He didn't say anything, just stared at her. When Pam said "Hello, there," the boy ran into another room and disappeared.

The Frenches haven't seen their friendly, mischievous, young ghost for sometime, though they feel his presence in the house. Pam believes that once the boy had met them and found out that they were nice people to live with, he was content to stay in the shadows and from time to time play little jokes by moving small items when she wasn't looking.

They have lived in the house for twenty-five years and each Halloween they purchase candy in anticipation—and still no trick-or-treaters have come to their door.

Children are afraid to go to the house on Halloween because it's supposed to be haunted by the ghost of a young boy.

Photo by Pam French

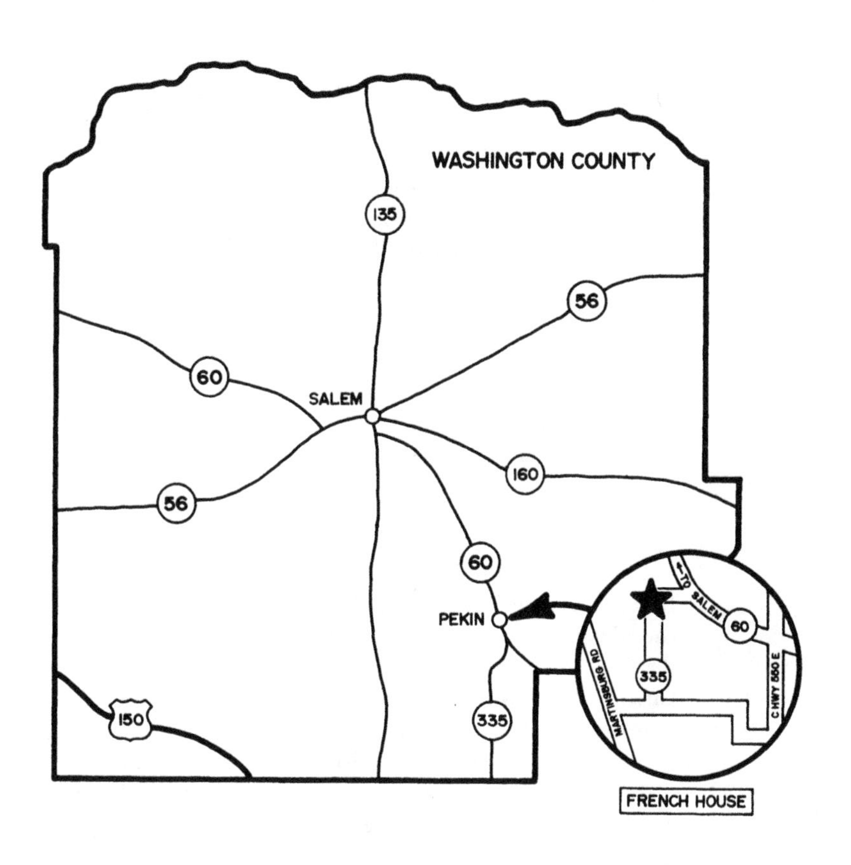
WASHINGTON COUNTY
135
56
60
SALEM
160
56
60
PEKIN
335
150
← TO SALEM
60
MARTINSBURG RD
335
C HWY 550 E
FRENCH HOUSE

Books of Interest

More Haunted Hoosier Trails
Folklore from Indiana's Spookiest Places
By Wanda Lou Willis

Beloved Indiana folklorist Wanda Lou Willis is back with all-new ghostly tales in this hair-raising companion to her popular *Haunted Hoosier Trails*. Set off with Wanda as your guide to explore Indiana's hidden history in even more spooky locations around the state. Local history buffs will relish the informative county histories that begin each chapter, while thrill-seekers will eagerly search out these frightening locations. *More Haunted Hoosier Trails* is perfect year-round for raising goose bumps around the campfire or reading under the covers with a flashlight.

Paperback Price $14.99
ISBN: 1-57860-182-7

Ghosthunting Ohio
Part of the Haunted Heartland series
By John Kachuba

Follow John Kachuba from the safety of your armchair as he explores eerie locations throughout Ohio. You'll visit the Majestic Theatre in Chillicothe, where Army victims of the 1918 Spanish influenza epidemic were "stacked like cordwood"; the Cincinnati Art Museum, home to at least three ghosts—one of whom is a seven-foot-tall medieval monk; Ft. Meigs in Perrysburg, where an invisible soldier accompanies employees to their cars at night; and twenty-nine other hair-raising locations around the state. And if the "spirit" moves you, you can check the Travel Guide at the back of the book for all the information you need to see each site for yourself.

Paperback Price $14.99
ISBN: 1-57860-181-9

Also available: *Ghosthunting Illinois* by John Kachuba

To order call: 1 (800) 343-4499 www.clerisypress.com
Clerisy Press 1700 Madison Road Cincinnati, Ohio 45206